Trail Guide for a Crooked Heart

"In our Hawaiian language, "Ike pono' can mean to see clearly, justly, truthfully, precisely. While no single author can answer all the queries of life, Jim May provides a lens for the reader to search for truth in the wisdom of story."

—Nyla Fujii-Babb, Native Hawaiian Storyteller

"Jim May links the mythic and the earthly together with a rich blend of personal yet universal insights, philosophy, humor, and an abundance of engaging narratives. It's a book that asks to be read over and over again."

—Doug Elliott, storyteller, author, and Appalachian naturalist

"The way a farmer hoes: attuned to proper season, just the right depth, choosing ready earth, seeding discerningly; that's how Jim May writes."

—Megan Wells, storyteller and author

"In these pages, you will find a near-perfect weaving of the mythic into the personal, following the voices from mentors: philosophers, humorists, and storytellers. Jim May convinces us that we need stories now more than ever. He presents stories we need today, stories that connect us to each other, to our ancestors and to those who will stand on our shoulders. If stories are medicine I want Jim as my doctor. The author Nabokov said a great story must entertain, instruct and enchant. In these pages, Jim May hits the trifecta. Part of Jim May's genius is his ability to engage farm families and boards of major corporations—and have them laughing, sobbing, and nodding in agreement at the same time."

—Kevin Kling, author, humorist, and occasional NPR commentator

"You can't beat spending time with a relaxed, smart, caring storyteller who can bring life to just about any incident from his past, throwing in clever wordplay, punch lines, and germane quotations—Nietzsche on love, for instance—to boot."

—NUVO WEEKLY

"Jim May has been inspiring students and colleagues (including myself) for almost four decades; this book will inspire a new generation to set out on their own journeys of discovery and invention. *Trail Guide For a Crooked Heart* is a powerful fusion of narrative and commentary that will encourage the reader to accept the challenge of perceptive storytelling. Struggling with a story on a deeply personal level has always been one of the fundamental challenges of being human. Jim May is one of the pioneers of American personal storytelling. This book shows how his adventure started, and why it continues so forcefully. Jim May is an American treasure."

—Ed Stivender, storyteller, educator, and author

"The overarching traits shared by Scottish Traveller Duncan Williamson and his friend, the American storyteller Jim May, must be a generosity of spirit and a kindness of the heart, expressed in each man's storytelling and in this book."

—Linda Williamson, Scottish folklore scholar, author, and widow of Duncan Williamson

Trail Guide for a
Crooked Heart

Stories and Reflections for Life's Journeys

> "Love Your Crooked Neighbour
> with Your Crooked Heart."
> —W.H. Auden,
> *As I Walked out One Evening*[1]

Jim May

**PARKHURST
BROTHERS
PUBLISHERS**

Parkhurst Brothers Publishers
MARION, MICHIGAN

www.parkhurstbrothers.com

Parkhurst Brothers books are distributed to the trade through the Chicago Distribution Center, and may be ordered through Ingram Book Company, Baker & Taylor, Follett Library Resources and other book industry wholesalers. To order from Chicago Distribution Center, phone 1-800-621-2736 or send a fax to 800-621-8476. Copies of this and other Parkhurst Brothers Inc., Publishers titles are available to organizations and corporations for purchase in quantity by contacting Special Sales Department at our home office location, listed on our website. Manuscript submission guidelines for this publishing company are available at our website.

Printed in the United States of America

2016 2017 2018 2019 2020   16 15 14 13 12 11 10 9 8 7 6
5 4 3 2

Library of Congress Cataloging-in-Publication Data

May, Jim, 1947- author.
 Trail guide for a crooked heart : stories and reflections for life's journeys / Jim May; with an Introduction by Jay O'Callahan—First edition.
      pages cm
 Includes bibliographical references.
 ISBN 978-1-62491-022-7 -- ISBN 978-1-62491-023-4 (ebk)
 1. May, Jim, 1947- 2. Conduct of life. 3. Storytellers. I. Title.
 BJ1589.M29 2015
 170'.44--dc23
                              2015013953

Parkhurst Brothers Publishers believes that the free and open exchange of ideas is essential for the maintenance of our freedoms. We support the First Amendment to the United States Constitution and encourage our fellow citizens to study all sides of public policy questions, making up their own minds. Closed minds cost a society dearly.

Cover art from a painting by   Nan Seidler
Cover photo of Jim May by   Harold Rail
Cover and interior design by   Linda D. Parkhurst, PhD
Proofread by   T. Percival Lamott
Acquired for Parkhurst Brothers Publishers and edited by Ted Parkhurst

All URLs in this book are being provided as a convenience and for informational purposes only; they do not constitute an endorsement or an approval by the publisher of any of the products, services or opinions. Parkhurst Brothers Publishers bears no responsibility for the accuracy, legality or content of linked sites or for that of subsequent links. Contact external sites for answers to questions regarding their content.

032016

I dedicate this book to

I love you more

and

My pen pal on the Queen's Esplanade

Contents

"If we don't know our own story well, in its darkness as well as its light, we can not know the story of 'the other' in its fullness. And if we can not empathize imaginatively with other people's stories, how much can we know about the real news of the world?"

—Thomas Merton[2]

> "Studied alive ... myth is not an explanation in satisfaction of a scientific interest, but a narrative resurrection of a primeval reality, told in satisfaction of deep religious wants, and moral cravings."
>
> —Bronislaw Malinowski,
> *Magic, Science, and Religion*

Introduction

Jim May has myth running through his veins. Myth, story, and imagination are as much a part of his life as his family, friends, community, and the land itself—Jim is restoring prairie and woodland on his land in Northern Illinois. He's a man of vision and as I read this book, I felt I was walking through the great doors of myth, and realized this is a book we all need to read to expand our vision.

I'll tell you of a day visiting Jim May in Spring Grove, which is part of McHenry County in Illinois. Jim stopped the car, pointed across the street and said, "That's the house I grew up in. And just two houses over, that's St. Peter's Church." Jim went on, "As a boy I'd get up on dark winter mornings and head to St. Peter's to serve Mass. I'd stop and look at Venus, bright as the Star of David. The church was cold and dimly lit. Father Fritz was frugal with the heat and the pleasantries." Jim described the two or three lonely people bundled up in the church like

"Dickens' characters."

Even as a boy Jim had one foot in the community—in this case, an old priest and two or three lonely parishioners, and the other foot in the stars. He was aware of Venus, aware of its beauty, aware that he was part of something vast, the universe. He had the eye of a poet and that's why his writing is often so lyrical.

As we went on with our tour of McHenry County, he told stories. We passed a library reminding Jim of Ray Bradbury's story *Fahrenheit 451*. Ray Bradbury's hometown, Waukegan, Illinois, is just down the road from the community where Jim grew up.

Fahrenheit 451 is a futuristic novel in which all books were supposed to be burned. Jim told that story for half an hour from memory.

Driving down a hill, we passed a construction site that reminded Jim of his brother, Paul, who broke into the trades as a heavy equipment operator and then founded his own company. Jim confided that his brother was the best storyteller in town.

Before starting his own company, Paul was head blade man (motor grader operator) for an excavation company. He got Jim a summer job there. Jim stayed on to pay his way through college.

On summer days, while on the dirt crew, Jim would see dust rising from all the heavy equipment headed down to the tree where Paul had parked his grader to eat his lunch. The men gathered there to hear his stories. He made them laugh like no one else could.

When we got to Jim's home that night, we began talking about the political issues of the day: climate change, immigration, the war in Afghanistan. We sat at the dining room table and Jim said, "Let me tell you the story of Percival and the Fisher King."

Jim told that story so intensely that I felt I was living it, and I was stunned by Percival's question at the end of the story, "What ails thee?" It was such a simple question, but it was the answer all along. Many of life's big questions can be whittled down to the answer to this small and seemingly insignificant question, "What ails thee?" which translates to, "Tell me your story."

I've related some of the incidents of the day because they reflect the power of this book. Jim May knows the importance of community and the importance of story, myth, and imagination to deepen our relationships and heal our world. The matter before us is—can we open our imagination wide enough to approach these tasks?

—Jay O'Callahan

Author of *Forged In The Stars*, a story of space exploration commissioned for NASA's 50th anniversary

Prologue

While growing up, I had often heard workers and tradesmen say that *it goes faster if you start.*

In spite of being raised among these industrious and shrewd farmers, horse traders, and construction workers in a working-class, Midwestern town, getting this book to press has taken me at least twelve years. So, all in all, I've been:

slower than sun on a wall,

as I once heard an old blacksmith say. I have been lucky to be raised in a farm family and working class community, privileged to be surrounded by language rich in regional dialect and metaphor, language untainted by the blandness that formal education too often imposes.

I also grew up in the Roman Catholic religion. Many of my queries about the nature of the divine were answered with,

It's a mystery, my son.

The older I get, the more I appreciate the mysterious nature of existence, and the more I appreciate the spiritual lives of many of my guiding teachers, my mentors.

Many of the stories in this book ponder the mystery that the light and the shadow dance together, and that the good and the bad somehow support each other. Therefore, I hope there may have been some virtue in my sloth.

I suppose, putting my best foot forward, I could offer that I have heeded the wisdom of taking my time and doing the task right the first time: *measure twice, cut once.* Or, that taking my time to complete the task has allowed the gathering of stories from far and wide, and perhaps, added a certain seasoning to these tales and observations. I hope this to be the case.

Over the years, my students and other listeners have approached me with gratitude when one of the stories that they heard me tell had been a help or inspiration to them. I have experienced this response as a teacher, as a college counselor, and as a full-time storyteller now for the last twenty-eight years.

I have more than an inkling that what these listeners have told me is true. Some of the stories in this volume, such as "The Man Whose Horse Ran Off" and the Baal Shem Tov story of brokenness, have virtually saved my life more than once. I have been revived by these stories when I was filled with regret or self-loathing, and out of touch with life's joys and treasures.

Finally, the stories that make us laugh are, perhaps, the most healing of all.

So, I offer these stories, reflections, and bits of wisdom, as some of the best of what I have heard in about half a lifetime. I hope they broadcast like good seeds landing upon souls where laughter, tears, or a satisfied curiosity may bring solace and even joy.

Some of these stories have been fashioned from my life. I have collected others with determined intent. Some stories were gifted to me by many of the greatest storytellers and oral tradition-bearers in the English-speaking world—for instance, as I sat listening to Duncan Williamson, a tradition-bearer in Scotland who was reported to know three thousand stories,[3] next to a coal-burning fireplace, a gale off of the North Sea howling at the door; or as I sat listening to a story next to a woodstove on an Appalachian Mountaintop, transfixed by Ray Hicks,[4] considered, at the time, to be the greatest living teller of the Appalachian Jack Tales.

Some of these stories were told to me by elders—wisdom keepers who had led extraordinary lives: who had known a queen, or survived a great war. I heard many more from regular folks, in my native McHenry County and elsewhere, who have simply gone about their daily labor, and who have tried to live their lives with integrity and humor.

Some of these stories have stuck to my socks as I wandered down my own crooked path, though they did not reveal themselves to me until my life had caught up with their wisdom.

Don't Believe Everything You Read
How to Read This Book

A storytelling colleague and friend, the late Gamble Rogers, used to warn storytellers,

Let the story speak for itself.

This is a noble creed, to be sure. Traditional myths and folk tales, in particular, have been preserved by humanity for centuries, in some cases without the benefit of written records, precisely because they stand on their own merit.

These cardinal stories have spoken to the survival of the people, often providing guidance and a moral code for living—a proper way to behave and treat one another in order that the tribe, the community would survive, prosper and flourish.

Then again there are great traditions of interpretation, such as the Hebrew Midrash, that view stories and spiritual teachings as fluid, changing their meaning and teaching when applied to various new circumstances, insights, scholarship, and points of view.

I have gained much, I believe, from listening to and reading commentary from the likes of Michael Meade, Laura Simms,[5]

Belden Lane, Gioia Timpanelli,[6] Joseph Campbell, Rollo May, Clarissa Pinkola Estés, and others, as they have wrestled with and speculated upon the great tales and myths of the human experience.

Their commentaries allow the reader and listener not only to better understand a story, but also support the notion that each of us can add our own, individual perspective to the enduring stories that have guided humankind. These scholars remind us that traditional stories have echoed down through the corridors of history in part because our prescient ancestors knew that we might find them useful, that the universal truths presented might be helpful in the context of our own lives.

I believe that the stories in this book can stand on their own. However, in some cases, I have added commentary, and so I leave it up to you, the reader, to consider the stories with, or without my perspective.

Or, you might read the story, think about it for awhile, maybe even put the book down for a time as the story makes its way into your own life, onto your own path, and then read my commentary later.

And, above all, if the story escapes you or makes little sense, let it go for now and read on. Maybe come back to it at another time in your life.

I once heard poet, scholar, teacher, and leader of men, Robert Bly,[7] speak at the Chicago Men's Conference. Addressing a large gathering of those eager to hear his wisdom, he led off his remarks promising that he would be commenting on matters that he had studied and thought about his whole life—matters of myth, and of spirit, and of politics, and of men.

I have some ... brilliant ideas to share—really good stuff ... and about half of these ideas represent my very best thinking; and about half is bullshit. Unfortunately, he said, I can't tell the difference. So that is your job.
—Robert Bly

Like the old man in the Hasidic tale that you will find later in this volume, Robert Bly here plays the part of the humble elder/leader who does not trespass upon the intelligence of the apprentice or colleague. Bly knows the slippery and protean nature of truth, and the dangers of a truth too tightly held.

So enjoy these stories and commentary if you like, but be wary as you read on, especially of anything that a storyteller, whether ancient or contemporary, seems to hold most sacred.

Chapter 1

Setting Out

Be Not Afraid[1]

The old monk awakened in his cave on the side of the mountain. The night's drowsiness slowly passed as his surroundings began to take shape. His consciousness emerged like the fog slowly being burned off by the sun low on the horizon. Looking out over the tree canopy, he smiled as he watched the mist rising and the birds welcoming the day with their songs and flutter.

Alert now, he became aware of the sound of something behind him in the far recesses of the cave: a low, muffled breathing, and scraping of claws on the wet stones.

The monk began to tremble, realizing that something had entered the cave while he had slept.

I am being stalked, he thought.

Indeed, whatever creature had invaded his simple domicile made its way closer and closer until he could feel its hot breath on his back and hear the low, hungry rumbling of a great stomach, poised to devour him.

Shaking, the old monk turned to face his demon. And there, not more than a few feet at his back, was a fierce beast, its eyes red and glowing, its claws pawing the air, a terrible stink emitting from its every pore.

"Oh," said the monk, "it's only you again."

Seek the Right Path[2]

A story from the Hasidic tradition tells of a young man on a journey through a dense forest.

Having traveled a great distance, he found himself lost. But he had three days' worth of provisions and felt confident that he would find his way home, for he was an experienced traveler. He continued walking, searching, attempting to reestablish his bearings.

However, at the end of the first day he found himself back where he first set out. He had lost a whole day, and worse, had consumed a day's worth of rations. Still surprised at his apparent miscalculation, he determined to be more careful.

On the morning of the second day he rose, rationed his now two days of food and water, and began anew. At the end of this second day, he found himself back at the same place from which he embarked two days before.

How could I have taken the wrong path two days in a row? He wondered.

So he set out the third day, paying close attention to every landmark, every boulder and streambed. But again, he somehow found himself back at his same starting point. He was out of food and water.

In desperate resignation, he prepared himself to die.

As darkness approached, he sat, head on his chest, thinking of his family, his friends, his dreams.

Then there came a rustling of footsteps and a dry, whispery greeting. He raised his head to see an old man walking toward him. A curious figure, moving with a slow, uneven gait, but his wrinkled face was radiant. The young man leaped to his feet.

"Whoever you are, it's a miracle that you've come. I need your help."

"Yes, yes, I am here, my son. Do not worry."

"But, I'm lost in these woods."

"Yes, yes, I know, but do not be alarmed; I am here to guide you."

"I've been lost in these woods for three days!"

The old man became more serious and then he brightened.

"Do not worry my son. All is well. You see, I have been lost for three years."

"Oh No!" shouted the young man as he collapsed in a hopeless swoon.

No, no it will be fine. It is true that I do not know the correct path out of this forest, but I know all of the paths that do not lead out of this forest.

Pack a Lunch

On any journey we take in life, chances are that we will sometimes need to rely on our inner reserves, rather than upon the current acclaim or nourishment from our family, community, or the world at large.

On any hiking trail—and in any life—there may be barren patches where the foraging does not bear fruit or much of anything else of nourishment. As we negotiate the barren places, bumps, and potholes of the human condition, we may find ourselves feeling empty or even lost.

In looking at our journeys as soul travel and initiatory[3] tasks for our continually evolving spirits, there are surely times of self-doubt, fear, and feelings of vulnerability.

Memories, stories, and meditations on how we have been loved can provide powerful support during these times of discouragement.

Stories that conjure up memories and images of our being loved, our acceptance into the family, among friends, or in our community, can bring comfort and strength during times of emotional drought. Most families have at least one oft-repeated story whose moral, if it were stated, would be something like this:

Life is hard, but here, in the family—or community—you know

you are loved, that we take care of one another.

Though these memories and anecdotes may be few, to focus on even the one and only time that we were well-loved, even for a moment, can sustain a lifetime. As an addendum, it should be considered that even if we have no memories of being loved, we can still act as if we do—and that we always *have the power to love.*

A teacher of mine used to tell a story about the lonely orphan who attached a note to a brick and threw it over the orphanage wall. These words were written on the note:

Whoever finds this, I love you.

A Day of Birth Story

Remembering the loving and humorous family stories told about the day of our birth or adoption can sustain us for years to come, sometimes through the most difficult circumstances. The day a newborn or new family member is welcomed is often a day of great joy that can lend perspective for a lifetime.

My sister Georgia was the firstborn of our family. Then came my brother Paul, the first boy born in our family. As he grew up, he wanted a baby brother. My mother's next baby was my sister Donna.

But Paul wanted a little brother. The next child to come along in our family was my sister, Diane. Still, there was no brother.

Then eight years passed as my brother, no doubt, gave up hope. But we were a Catholic family and there was one more *rhythm baby* in the offing. My mother used to say that the priest would tell the parishioners,

... a baby a year, and in a good year, two.

My brother was twelve when I was born. We lived on a farm on Grass Lake Road about five miles east of the village of Spring Grove, Illinois. The call came from the hospital that my mother had given birth, at last, to a brother for Paul.

According to the family legend, Paul rode his bicycle five miles on a gravel road, up and down hills, over bumps and wash-boarded hard pack into Spring Grove so he could tell aunts and uncles there that he had a baby brother. What's more, he accomplished this feat on his old, broken-down bike, *with a flat tire.*

From my earliest memories to this very moment of recalling and writing, whenever I've heard this story, often repeated when family gathered as I was growing up, I knew that my big brother loved me, and that he would look out for me.

Paul, in fact, got me the union construction job that allowed me to pay my way through college after our father had died. He often offered advice on family matters, taking responsibility off of my shoulders. Once he told me that our late father would be proud of my entry into college, the first of my family. When my mother was ill and I considered leaving the University of Illinois, Paul took me aside and said to concentrate on my studies, that I had to live my own life. I knew that he was assuring me that mom would be ok.

Likewise, when we were growing up, the bike story became especially important when I was convinced that my brother was trying to kill me and drive me crazy—as brothers are wont to do.

My earliest memories, I must have been four or five, include my brother convincing me that a wolf lived in my parents' bedroom (Sigmund Freud eat your heart out). At the time, we lived in an old farmhouse on Tryon Grove Road in Richmond, Illinois. The house had a large bedroom downstairs off the living room. Our parents slept there. The rest of the family slept upstairs.

On many occasions, Paul played catch with me in the living room. Of course, I loved playing catch and I relished the attention from my brother. He'd lob the ball at me. Most times I missed it and had to give chase—run the ball down before I could throw it back to him. But I didn't mind. I loved playing ball with my brother.

Back and forth, throwing and catching, until I was in a state of delirious joy … And then, having played the game with me just long enough so that I had forgotten all about the beast in the adjacent room, at just the right moment, Paul would sail the ball into my parents' bedroom. I'd skip happily after it—well into the bedroom's far corner, searching for the frisky ball. After a few moments pause, as Paul waited to make sure I had journeyed to the far reaches of the bedroom—the wolf's lair—a blood-curdling scream would come from the living room behind me: Paul yelling with all his might:

Look out for the wolf!

It goes without saying, due to the inadequacies of traction applied by one's cotton socks upon the linoleum floor, that I suffered inert terror for several dreadful moments before I gained enough momentum to hurl myself out of the bedroom and into the kitchen to complain to my mother, crying and hiccuping the whole way.

During the early fifties, when I was six years old, Paul had me convinced that the United States Army was drafting little boys to go to the front lines in Korea to haul water to the troops.

After my mother found me crying in my bed, she made him stop and assured me that, while we must pray for the children and families to whom war was an everyday, ever present reality, I had nothing to worry about.

But these memories of teasing and terror fade alongside the birthday story of Paul's legendary bicycle trip—his spontaneous expression of sheer joy that I was born his brother.

> **" ... the birds of the air shall tell the truth ..."**
> —Ecclesiastes, Chapter 10, Verse 20

Chapter 2

My Own Journey
Storytelling, the Thing with Feathers

I'm a bird watcher. Actually, I call myself a birder because it sounds more masculine.

In the fall of 1978, I was teaching elementary school in Woodstock, Illinois. A happy teacher, I was minding my own business, when John, a birder friend and fellow teacher from a school district down the road, got into my ear about something called *storytelling*. He uttered the word, *storytelling*, with reverence, as if it was a specific, enchanting experience, set in place and time.

The single word seemed to hold a meaning for John that described a complete and mysterious adventure that he would return to each year, a pilgrimage to the mountains of Tennessee, the oldest mountains on earth, where, he promised, one could hear some of the oldest stories in the world.

John and I had traded teaching ideas and strategies—anything to get our students excited about learning: nighttime stargazing, math puzzles and games, and Readers Theater .... We enjoyed the camaraderie, and the collaborations seemed to benefit our students.

So I think John wanted to share something with me, something that he saw as amazing, and a little odd. His desire to share this new passion made sense because I had introduced him to bird watching.

John had spent most of his life thinking there were big birds like crows, hawks and eagles, and then there were sparrows. When I helped John to see the staggering variety of birdlife—species seemingly as numerous as the stars in the sky, with some individual species as varied and colorful as tropical fish—he took to birding with a passion. John shared his love of birding with his fifth graders, and eventually received an Environmental Teacher of The Year award.

In the fall of 1977 he had returned from a visit to The Okefenokee Swamp, America's largest fresh and black water wilderness wetland, which straddles the Georgia-Florida state line. John was doing some research there for an advanced degree. Driving back to the Chicago area through the breath-taking and majestic Smoky Mountains of Tennessee, he saw a sign, *storytelling*. John and his wife, Pat, were nothing if not curious adventurers, so they followed the sign's arrows.

When John and Pat got home they told me of a small town, Jonesborough, tucked away in the hills of Eastern Tennessee, the oldest settlement in the state, complete with two hundred-year-old brick buildings and an old courthouse bench originally occupied by whittlers and tale-tellers. Since 1972, thousands of people had traveled there every year to hear stories. The annual gathering turned into something called the National Storytelling Festival.

John told me he had already decided to return the following autumn, and he asked that I go with him. *Storytelling?* It seemed weird to me. Unconvinced, I turned down John's offer.

The Herald Call of Prairie Sirens

The following spring, John approached me again with another proposition. This time he invited me to accompany him and his fifth-grade class down to Effingham, Illinois, to witness the courtship ritual of the Greater Prairie Chicken.[1] *I packed my bags immediately!*

If you are disinterested in birds and/or nature, you can skip this part. BUT, *if you want to hear about the feathered "Sirens of the Prairie," the romantic superstars of the bird world, the acrobatic avian dancers from whom the native people learned some of their moves, and lastly, the feathered denizens of the prairie who acted as Herald Angels to my storytelling journey, then,* BY ALL MEANS, READ ON!

For centuries ten to fourteen million prairie chickens roamed the Illinois prairies. A scant few, a hundred or so, are left. In the spring of 1979 the only place to see them in Illinois was at the Prairie Ridge State Natural Area in Effingham, Illinois. And that is where John, his students, and I found ourselves the spring following his second autumn visit to the National Storytelling Festival.

We started the day at 4:00 a.m. in a barn converted into a nature center. There we sat in steel folding chairs as the Rangers from the Illinois Department of Natural Resources (DNR) briefed us on what we were about to see. These rare pairings of prairie chickens occur on what is called a *booming ground* or *lek*. Booming is the sound male prairie chickens produce during their communal courtship display.

Standing in the front of the room, wearing nylon bomber jackets and holding wooden pointers, the DNR boys drew our attention to diagrams of the booming grounds. Then they showed us pictures of the greater prairie chicken and the lesser prairie chicken. What about the underachieving *not so great* greater prairie chicken, I wondered, or for that matter, the pretty-great lesser? We all listened carefully, in solemn anticipation:

... birders at full alert.

The naturalists gave us real cool bird-science type jobs. We teachers were to carry clipboards, in order to count, every fifteen minutes, the number of males and females on the booming ground ... and the number of successful and unsuccessful copulations. Silence filled the room.

John and I looked at each other. Professional educators that we were, we immediately realized we needed more in-service training on the delicate subject of wild chicken love.

Responding to our questions, the DNR staff explained to us that there were three reliable indications of a successful prairie chicken mating:

1. *The encounter between male and female lasts about three seconds (be glad you are not a prairie chicken).*

2. *After a successful mating, the female steps a few feet away from the male, she ruffles her feathers.*

3. *She gives a little squawk—Aurk!*

Hidden in our blinds, we were to check the box on our clip-boards with the appropriate level of satisfaction all around. After all, this was an endangered species that we were about to witness so the completion of this procreative act was practically a kind of avian *Hallelujah* moment.

⁓

We were driven to the booming grounds in the dark. There we waited for the birds in the predawn. In our blinds, we shivered with cold and excitement. Then came the sound, ghostly and everywhere—a mournful, otherworldly, lovesick, plaintive cooing, like the sound of someone blowing across the mouth of an empty bottle.

As the sun-tinged, minty-cool, spring air slowly waded across the prairie, we began to see shapes emerging in the smoky light. From our blinds, the birds looked much smaller than their booming suggested. The first birds on the booming ground were the males, who marked and defined small patches of territory with a complex frolic of stomping, strutting, and twirling.

The purpose of this feisty claim-staking was to invite a female, to woo a mate.

The males inflated their orange air sacs (*tympani*), erected their black neck feathers (*pinnae*), stomped their feet, and emitted the three noted booming sounds, who-OOM-oom, which could be heard up to a mile away. They spun, cackled, and chased away other males, which they instinctively viewed as genetically inferior, with fierce intensity as if they knew their species was on the edge of extinction. After a time, the females arrived. With wings set, they landed soft as milkweed down onto the dewy, silvered grass.

If John, his students, and I doubted the males could move any faster or become more intense when the females arrived, boy-howdy, were we wrong!

Everything churned. The males shifted into high gear while the females casually pecked at a larva here, a seed there, as if pretending not to notice the frantic, staccato twirling, and booming of their suitors, orange neck sacs ballooned in their desperation to impress. When a female would venture onto a male's territory and sidle up, a male mounted her and the longed for, and carefully planned, act would be accomplished in the long blink of an eye. Unless, that is, from a nearby bachelor's lair, a jealous and ambitious male would charge the first amorous rival, and knock him from his carnal perch, sending him tumbling butt over crop. The daring interloper would then replace the startled male who sat, for a while, in a dreamy state before he shook himself off and got back on the dance floor.

John's fifth graders were riveted. Not one distraction arose. No one asked to get a drink of water, or go to the bathroom ... .

If all of this wasn't enough excitement, every hour or so a Northern Harrier (Marsh Hawk) or two dove down upon the whole flock, causing the little birds to flush and scatter across the prairie. After a few minutes, they would return in twos and threes, alighting back on the booming ground, and the whole avian extravaganza would begin again.

"When we returned to the nature center, I asked one of the DNR rangers how many missing and killed prairie chickens they attributed to the Marsh Hawks.

"Oh, the Harriers don't kill prairie chickens," he said.

Really?"

From his answer, I imagined two harriers dipping and bobbing along, low to the ground, in their unique, graceful flight pattern, talking to one another:

What ya wanna do?

I dunno know. What you wanna do?

Hey! I know! Let's go bushwhack those love-sick prairie chickens ... scare the poop out of 'em.

Great idea! Let's go!

Well, we had a wonderful time and felt fulfilled and pleased on the eight-hour bus ride home, in spite of the hoard of ticklish questions that John's fifth graders forced us to answer about what they had witnessed.

Later that summer John and I were chatting about our teaching experiences.

John proclaimed that two of the coolest things he'd ever done were accomplished in the last couple years.

"Really? What were they?"

"Well, there were the prairie chickens."

"I'd say!" I piped in.

"And the other ... *storytelling*."

I considered that if this *storytelling* thing could rank in the rarified air of those hormonally gifted prairie chickens, then I wanted in.

~~~

The National Storytelling Festival

The following fall of 1979 I found myself listening to stories at the seventh annual National Storytelling Festival in Jonesborough, the oldest town in Tennessee.

I heard storytellers of all descriptions. Ron Evans, of the Métis[2] people of Canada, a First Nation aboriginal tribe, described himself as the *Keeper of the Talking Sticks*—the official storyteller of his community.

I heard a retired commercial sea captain from the Maine coast who told of lobstermen, storms at sea, and of shipping out *down east (downwind)* from Cape Cod to Maine.

Kathryn Windham,[3] of Alabama, the first woman journalist in the state, had carefully researched her home state's many ghosts and spoke of them with heartbreaking eloquence, and even affection.

Most remarkable were the local Appalachian storytellers[4] who had come down to the festival to tell stories, some of which were told in language and lilts that reflected centuries-old patterns of English and Scots-Irish speech. With a soft and welcoming cadence, these tellers brought stories to the festival as their ancestors might have delivered lumber on a mule cart to the old Jonesborough settlement.

When these mountain tellers spoke, it was as if their words welled up from the nearby hills and hollows. Some told ancient stories passed down for generations within their own families.

Their stories seemed to have ascended beyond the wood stoves and mud fireplaces of mountain homes to be netted and preserved, like the smoked hams that hung in many a kitchen— by a tradition, a way of life, with its own practices and beliefs, that kept the stories echoing through time, across the ridges, from one storyteller and generation to another.

These stories had not been learned in a school, for the most part, but in weathered wood-frame houses and cabins scattered throughout the mountains. The tales were told for entertain- ment, for their wisdom, and to keep the children working at the many tedious tasks, like shelling beans, that were necessary for survival.

Ray Hicks, tradition-bearer, and among the greatest ever of the Jack Tale-tellers, used to say:

The tales ease the heart.

In the obvious joy that these mountain storytellers derived from being in the company of listeners and other tellers, and in the sassy, homegrown flavor of their wit and wisdom, I recognized elements of my own upbringing in rural McHenry County, Illinois, where my mother graduated eighth grade and my father, born in 1896, finished *McGuffey's Third Eclectic Reader*[5] (which was written at a Junior High level) before he dropped out of school to work on his father's farm.

I'd worked on construction crews and horse farms, and in each of these jobs, met great storytellers, masters of humor and language who had very little of the formal education that tends to homogenize and wash out regional colloquialisms and metaphors, figures of speech and the like. Once a worker had proven himself sufficiently knowledgeable and reliable, and able to hold up his end of the daily grind, stories, jokes, anecdotes and turns of phrase bantered about on lunch breaks, and during the working day, would enhance his standing on the crew.

So, hearing these clever and poetic folk-telling mountain people gave me the inspiration and permission to look to my own background and my own family and community experiences for stories to tell.

Jack Tales

Whether it be "Jack and the Beanstalk," "Jack and the Northwest Wind," "Soldier Jack," or a tale about one of Jack's other escapades, these stories compose an American cycle of hero-trickster tales featuring an innocent, kind-hearted, though sly and resourceful, character named Jack. Jack always makes his way through life, always on the edge of survival, but filled with hope, humor and compassion, and, most of all, adventure and wit.

Over the years, I have made acquaintance with the Ray Hicks Family of Beech Mountain, North Carolina. The Hicks family, along with their kinfolk, the Ward family, the Harmon family, and the Gentry family, were the primary preservers and transmitters of the Jack Tale Cycle in America. Ray Hicks was an eighth generation storyteller in his family, the patriarch of the Appalachian Jack Tale tradition, and recipient of a National Endowment Heritage Fellowship.

These stories about Jack can be traced back to the origins of our western civilization, emanating from the experience of our European ancestors, and manifesting—gloriously—in the everyday life and stories of certain Appalachian people, whose families have continued to tell these stories down through the generations.

On that first Saturday morning, I wandered into the Tent in the Park, where the great Jackie Torrence, a powerful African-American teller, was *tellin' bout Jack.*

To my knowledge, though Jackie Torrence never claimed to have heard these Jack Tales in her family, she seemed to resonate with the character of Jack, the trickster, and hero—with every ounce of her being. Perhaps her experience as an African-American single mom had given her all the insight and grist she needed to mill an unforgettable version of Jack, the quintessential survivor, no matter the odds. Hearing Jackie Torrence that first Saturday morning, at my first storytelling festival, left me inspired to retell the story to my students. A fifth grader's developmental task is to survive childhood.

I returned to my elementary school teaching duties to face my fifth grade students with a hundred stories from my weekend still whispering in both ears.

I told my class the one story that I actually remembered, an old mountain tale, "Soldier Jack,"[6] that I had heard from Jackie Torrence. It was the first story that I heard that weekend at the Tent in the Park festival location.

I began:

Jack quit the king's army, because he was tired of fightin' folks that he didn't even know— just 'cause the king was mad at 'em. So Jack set out to seek his fortune ...

Within minutes every set of eyes in my classroom was transfixed. It was not so much that they were looking at me; there was a dreaminess about my students' gaze as they *watched* the cinema-like scenes that were playing out in their imaginations. Perhaps, at first, they were thinking:

What happened to our teacher over the weekend? He's a lot more interesting than he was last Friday afternoon.

However, within minutes, there seemed to be nothing in the room but Jack and his adventures. My role as teacher had melted away. There was no need for discipline or a precise strategy for presenting a lesson about use of language, the function of descriptive phrasing, or the power of laughter to add dynamic impact to any narrative.

My students and I were fellow travelers, like pilgrims on the way to Canterbury, each with our own interest in Jack's survival and success. The story that I told, "Soldier Jack," like so many stories passed down through the millennia, had all the touch points that animate the trials and joys of the human condition, whether one is ten years old or eighty.

I knew something very important was happening. Why? Because in my ten years of teaching—until that very moment—I had never experienced such complete attention and focus from my students.

After what seemed like a moment later, but was really more like twenty minutes, the story ended:

> **... and the Death Angel took Jack, but he had lived a long and happy life.**

With the story done, my students wanted *more stories*. Having only a weekend's exposure to this new thing called storytelling I only knew one story. So I set out to learn more.

> *I had embarked upon a new journey.*

> **"The most important of divine grace often comes in a form we would never choose had we the choice."**
> —Belden Lane, *The Solace of Fierce Landscapes*

Chapter 3

Broken and Blessed

Windows For The Soul

The stuff of our own lives, the human condition, tends to be complex, unedited, often paradoxical and filled with surprises, unexpected joys, tragedies, and peculiar predicaments. If we took the first step into adulthood or any other first step in life, thinking that our life would always stay on a straight, easily navigated path, we would surely have been mistaken.

So, it is fortunate that timeless, traditional stories—and storytellers—reassure us that both hardships and mistakes can lead to transformation. Cinderella, the one with the most pain and loss in her life, becomes the princess. Beauty loves the Beast, and it is always the old, raggedy woman alongside the road who knows more about getting the queen pregnant than the king does.

Johnny Moses[1]—storyteller, traditional healer, and a spiritual leader of his people, was born in a village of the Nuu-chah-nulth (Nootka) tribe of Vancouver Island, British Columbia. I once heard him say, at one of his teaching workshops, that in his tribe,

**Mistakes are thought of as windows for the soul
to climb out of
in order to grow larger.**
—Johnny Moses

〜

We must learn from the mistakes of others because no one lives long enough to make enough of their own.[2]
—Eleanor Roosevelt

〜

The Cracked Pot[3]

There once was a young water carrier whose job it was to descend a steep hill each day, to fill up two large pots, and then to climb back up the hill, thus providing his village with water.

The pots hung on each side of a long stick that the young man balanced across his shoulders. His task proceeded daily for some years.

It so happened, that one of the two pots had a very small crack, an imperfection in the clay, and therefore this pot always lost some of its water in the journey up the hill.

Now, in these old teaching stories, sometimes animals, and even objects, could speak as if human.

Being virtuous and utilitarian, the little pot was quite saddened that she was not performing up to the standards of her neighbor—the pot on the other side of her master's stick. So one day she apologized to the water carrier for losing so much water over the days, weeks, months, and years of their common toil.

"Come with me little pot; I have something to show you."

The young man carried her out of the cottage, and down the path. There, on one side of the path, bloomed a row of lovely, colorful flowers, swaying in the summer breeze.

Honeybees by the score encircled the sweet blossoms—the scene being altogether one of great beauty and splendor.

"You see, little pot, each day the crack in your side provided enough water to nourish these beautiful flowers that have brought joy to my heart and allowed me to cheerfully continue my burdensome labor."

We often construct carefully thought-out plans for ourselves, our loved ones, our colleagues, and communities. We set goals and arrange our priorities. We try to manage our values and resources to match what we want to accomplish. We feel satisfied and rewarded when our goals are achieved.

But sometimes events sabotage our plans. We confront unexpected and even tragic circumstances. Confusion, grief, self-doubt, anger, and other understandable emotions may result and become overwhelming.

Our failures or missteps, or fate's random course, can be even more difficult to maneuver if we fail to see some—perhaps small—nugget of learning, or even good and beauty that may rise from misfortune.

Adversity, or even tragedy, perhaps can be better endured if we can see some benefit arising from tribulation.

A dramatic case in point: in 1978 the American Nazi Party marched in Skokie, Illinois—the US community with the largest population of Jewish Holocaust Survivors. This outrageous act of hatred and disrespect for the suffering and death of millions of Jews during World War II drew bitter opposition, of course.

Outraged by the presence of Nazis parading in their community, by the display of Swastikas in their neighborhood ... Holocaust Survivors who had never spoken in public of their WWII experience came out to tell their stories in schools, synagogues, churches and throughout the community. These stories are being told to this very day.

Likewise, the Nazi march is credited with the impetus to build the 65,000 square foot Illinois Holocaust Museum and Education Center that opened in Skokie on April 19, 2009—a culmination of thirty years of hard work by the local Holocaust survivor community and supporters.[4]

According to President Emeritus Sam Harris,

"We dreamt of creating a place that would not only serve as a memorial to our families that perished and the millions lost, but also where young minds could learn the terrible dangers of prejudice and hatred."

To ensure that young people continue to learn these lessons, the organization successfully secured the 1990 passage of the Holocaust Education Mandate, making Illinois the first state to require Holocaust Education in public schools.

In 2005, the organization was again influential in expanding this mandate; the Holocaust and Genocide Education Mandate now requires Illinois schools to teach about all genocides.

It is noteworthy to add that the First Amendment's Free Speech clause of the US Constitution prevailed here. The American Civil Liberties Union (ACLU) defended the Nazi's right to march based on the principal that in the free exchange of ideas, no matter how repugnant that some of those ideas may be, truth will eventually carry the day.

Though we may wish our life to resemble a straight road, with a predictable landscape presenting only manageable bumps, learning to survive—and even prosper—on our real paths, *our crooked paths*, prepares us to appreciate and cope with life's vagaries, surprises, and challenges.

Life is what happens while we are making other plans.
—John Lennon[5]

A Baal Shem Tov Story[6]

Rabbi Yisrael ben Eliezer, also known as the *Baal Shem Tov*, or (*Besht*), or Master of the *Good Name* (of God) was an influential Jewish mystical rabbi, born in Eastern Europe around 1700. He is considered to be the founder of Hasidic Judaism. He became very knowledgeable in the Kabbalah and other important teachings of the Jewish religion, and traveled widely with his disciples bringing the teachings in the form of stories to the common people. Filled with wisdom and compassion, the stories have endured through the centuries.

It is said that at a time of great threat upon the Jewish community, The Baal Shem Tov had gathered his disciples to pray for deliverance.

The master singled out a particular disciple, beseeching him to pray with more resolve and intensity. The disciple heeded the Baal Shem Tov's exhortation, trying his best to somehow pray with more conviction, more compassion, perhaps more humility, even striking his breast and crying out.

But the Baal Shem Tov grew angry, telling the disciple:

Your miserable prayers are not being heard. How can you not ascend to greater devotion in this hour of need?

Over and over again the master berated the disciple until the man threw himself on the floor in a fit of sobbing and pleading.

When he finally had composed himself, the disciple resumed his prayers and, in fact, found new words with which to pray.

The threat passed. The people were delivered. However the disciple, still humiliated and feeling betrayed, approached the Baal Shem Tov to ask why he had treated him so harshly. The master replied that,

When the bonds between heaven and earth are in grave danger what's needed is more than prayer—what's needed is words from a broken heart.

The Man Whose Horse Ran Off

In ancient China there lived an old man who farmed a small rice paddy with his only son and their horse. Each year, the two of them and their horse prepared, planted, and harvested the rice.[7]

Despite all of their hard work, their rice paddy was so small that after harvest each year they had just enough rice for a meager serving each day, a small amount to replant, and a bit to barter.

One day, the horse ran off. The neighbor who had learned of this tragedy visited them.

"What will you do now?" he asked. "You have no way to plant your rice. You will starve."

The old man replied,

I do not know if this is good or bad.

Weeks later, the horse returned with a wild mate. The neighbor stopped by to rejoice:

"You have doubled your wealth, now you can plant more rice, and have enough to sell for gold. Then you can rent more land, and plant even more rice, earn even more gold, and someday be a rich man!"

The old man said again:

I do not know if this is good or bad.

During its training the wild horse trampled the son, causing him to lose the use of his legs. Each night the old man sat up nursing his son, who lay on a mat, writhing in pain.

After the accident, when the neighbor would visit, the old man would greet him with tears in his eyes. Then, while the two sat keeping vigil by the boy, the old man would say to his faithful friend,

Even this could be good or bad.

As the story comes to an end, a warlord is assembling a great army at the edge of the province in which the old man, his son, and the neighbor live. All of the young men in the village are marching off to face certain death at the hands of an overwhelmingly superior force.

It is a matter of honor that they participate in this waste of human life.

The neighbor, bound by duty, embraces his sons and sends them off to die. Then, with grief laden steps, he travels to visit the old man whose son had recovered enough to work in the rice paddy with his father, but, with his profound limp, was unable to join the army.

"How fortunate you are," said the neighbor, "to have your son's company in your old age."

To this, the old man replied,

I do not know if this is good or bad.

Some say that, to this day, in China, a friend may greet your good fortune or personal tragedy with the words:

I hear your horse ran off.

Back in the days when I was a college counselor, this was the first story I heard my students referencing when they shared which of the stories that I told had helped them through difficult life experiences.

In the Hollywood movie, *Charlie Wilson's War*, the CIA operative, played by Phillip Seymour Hoffman, repeatedly asks the congressman from Texas, Charlie Wilson, played by Tom Hanks, if he'd like to hear a Zen story—this while the two of them are secretly carrying out an operation to send sophisticated weapons to the mujahideen who were fighting the invading Russians in Afghanistan.

The congressman fends off the story throughout the movie protesting that:

He did not have time *for a story* because, "We're fightin' the Russians!"

But, at the end of the movie, when Charlie Wilson and the CIA agent are toasting the victory of the mujahideen over the Russians, Charlie Wilson finally lets the CIA agent tell the story.

The story that the CIA agent tells is "The Man Whose Horse Ran Off." From the point of view of the CIA and US foreign policy, the good was the defeat of the Russians. The bad became the strengthening of the mujahideen jihadists, some of whom later became Al Qeada and brought about the eventual tragedy of Sept 11, 2001—the destruction of the World Trade Center towers in New York City.

Was our support of the mujahideen good or bad?

Abraham Lincoln—Our Greatest Broken Leader

Some have written that Lincoln suffered from melancholy and depression for most of his life.

In the book, *Lincoln's Melancholy: How Depression Challenged a President and Fueled His Greatness,* author Joshua Wolf Shenk writes that Lincoln's determination to end slavery, his great sorrow for the loss of life during the Civil War, and his historic intention to forgive the Confederacy after he led the Union army to victory, were positions that he held in deference to his own familiarity with pain, and the dark nights of the human spirit.

> **"What's essential is invisible to the eye."**
> *The Little Prince*
> Antoine de Saint-Exupéry

Chapter 4

The Third Eye—Seeing the Unseen[1]

The Peddler of Swaffham and His Dream

Once, a kind and humble peddler lived in the village of Swaffham, in Norfolk, England.[2] He traveled from village to village with a peddler's pack of wares, selling small household items, a few pretty things, and toys for the children. Trading and peddling were his life's work.

In his later years he began to worry about his old age. He had no children or wife to care for him and he had not saved his money, for his heart usually got in the way of him earning a good living.

Once, a little girl with bare feet, and a torn dress, picked out a delicate, crimson ribbon from the peddler's pack. Avoiding the peddler's eyes, she tied up her dirty hair with the ribbon and began to twirl, and sing to herself.

When she learned the price of the ribbon, her face fell. She placed the ribbon back in the peddler's hand and began to walk away, chin on her bony chest.

"Wait!" said the Peddler.

That ribbon would certainly rather dance with you than linger in my sack. It will miss you if you leave it with me. I will not have such a sad ribbon weighing me down with its tears. Please take it ... my gift.

The little girl's face burst into a smile; she grabbed the ribbon, and skipped off.

Another time a boy found a pennywhistle among the peddler's wares. He placed it to his lips and in a short time was able to play a bit of a lively tune. The peddler and two or three of the old women shopping in the market applauded his efforts.

But when the tune was done, the boy slowly placed the whistle back on the peddler's shabby rug, as if he did not wish to become too familiar with a joy that he could not afford.

"Boy, this whistle has been in my pack for weeks. I cannot sell it. Suppose you trade me whatever you have in your pocket."

For a fact, the peddler enjoyed sight unseen trades, and since he had traded many pennywhistles in his day he fancied himself the patron of a whole band of children filling their desperate lives with melody.

Offered a trade by the kind peddler, a boy or girl would eagerly stab their grimy little hands into a pocket to retrieve a shiny stone, a sea shell, or a frog.

The peddler would often think to himself that as long as he had his small cottage with a roof over his head, and his old cherry tree in the back yard to provide him shade, he could live well enough. Though, as the years passed, he became more fretful about his old age and how he might care for himself.

Then, one night, he dreamt that if he were to go to London and stand on London Bridge for three days, he would find a fortune that would secure him in his old age.

In the morning, he sat with his tea at his small table. As he gazed at the cherry tree in his back yard, he mulled over this curious dream, but dared not reckon that it had any importance.

His neighbor stopped by and they shared tea and visited. Just as the neighbor got up to leave, a flock of black birds (English Thrushes[3]) descended upon the cherry tree and began to feast upon the plump cherries.

"There they are again," scoffed the neighbor, "and, no doubt, you will let them have all they want of your cherries, as is you custom."

The peddler laughed, "Oh, I get a pie or two, but the blackbirds sing for me all the year through. I cannot think to deprive them of the tasty cherries when their song cost me nothing."

"You're kindhearted to be sure," chuckled the neighbor, "but a fool nonetheless. You could sell those cherries at the market, and the plump blackbirds as well, for that matter—a fine pie they would make."

That night the peddler was visited by the same dream—if he

would leave his cottage in Swaffham, travel to London Bridge, and stay for three days and nights, he would have his fortune.

The dream came again on the third night.

When the peddler awakened the morning after the third night he determined to set out for London, foolish though it seemed.

And there, on the bridge, among the bustle and commotion, he waited. One day passed, and then two days without event, and finally, three days and nights. On the morning of the fourth day, he set out for home, to return to Swaffham, his cherry tree, and his peddler's life.

But a butcher, who had a shop there on the bridge, saw him passing by. The butcher came out of his shop. "Peddler!" he shouted. "I have seen you here on the bridge for three days. You are here when I arrive at my shop in the morning and when I leave at night. You are not selling your wares or begging. What have you been doing?"

The peddler told the butcher of his dream—that if he waited on London Bridge for three days and three nights, he would find his fortune and be taken care of in his old age.

The butcher laughed:

"You are an old fool and a simpleton. You cannot make a fortune by sitting around and pondering your dreams. I work hard for my living. I am a man of action and commerce—I am here in my butcher shop early in the morning and I don't leave until sunset. I sell my meats for what they are worth and not a penny less. That's how I've made my fortune, what there is of it."

"In fact," continued the butcher, "I had a silly dream last night. I dreamt that if I traveled to the village of Swaffham, a place of which I've never heard, I would find a cottage there with a cherry tree in the backyard, a tree filled with blackbirds; and then, if I dug under that tree, I would find a fortune in buried pirates' gold.

Now, you don't see me dropping everything to travel to this Swaffham place to dig for gold do you?

"No, I don't," answered the peddler.

The peddler excused himself and returned home.

It is said that the kind, old peddler dug up a great fortune of gold buried under his cherry tree, that he lived a long, prosperous life, and that the good that he did with that gold for the children and all of his neighbors ... Well, that story would fill another book.

A Peddler's Teaching

In traveling through this world with its joys, sorrows, loves and losses, whether in the realm of our psyche or on foot, by car, or bus, train or airplane, there may be moments, minutes, or even days when time is compressed or seems to vanish altogether.

Have you ever driven your car for a while, then looked out the car window and thought:

Yes, I've arrived here, but how? I don't remember the turns, and how is it that I haven't crashed my car?

Concerning the forces that seem to take over our consciousness at these times, is it possible that the same subconscious energy that allows us to drive for miles and negotiate landscapes seemly without awareness, might be available to our lives in other ways as well?

Perhaps if we live our lives open to stories, to narratives, to symbolism, to art, and to myth, there is a chance that our subconscious, our intuition, and our ability to imagine, may emerge to inform our conscious mind.

I was once telling stories to a large group of second-graders in an auditorium. As they were all filing by the stage after the program, along came a boy in a bit of a hurry, jostling past me.

The second grader looked over his shoulder at me and said, "Thanks for the movies."

I don't think he was trying to be clever or metaphorical, but rather, telling me what transpired in his imagination: scenes with characters and action. It did not occur to him that they were not real movies.

The alternative to paying attention to our imaginations, our third eye, or window to the subconscious—or perhaps, to another dimension—is to see everything as true or false, right or wrong, science or fantasy.

Mark Twain's Third Eye

Mark Twain, in *Life On The Mississippi*, notes that the very process of mastering the knowledge required to be a riverboat pilot hastened his loss of poetic vision in matters concerning the river that he loved:

Now when I had mastered the language of this water and had come to know every trifling feature that bordered the great river as familiarly as I knew the letters of the alphabet, I had made a valuable acquisition.

**But I had lost something, too.
I had lost something which could never be restored to me while I lived.**

All the grace, the beauty, the poetry had gone out of the majestic river!
—Mark Twain, *Life On The Mississippi*

Often, when I'm telling stories in elementary schools, a young child will ask:

Is that story true?

It seems that from a young age on we are encouraged, perhaps pressured, to build a wall between the real world and the imaginary world, the world of matter and the world of spirit, the world of reason verses that of intuition.

Children asking me the question above want to know on which side of the wall to put a recounting of factual events like my farm story, "Bootsie, the Cattle-Herding Chihuahua" or a folk or fairy tale.

And so, from a young age, most of us trudge along, moored to our factual universe. But, even if we don't have a religious or spiritual belief, life happens to us and within us. We long for a loved one who has died. We seek to escape the perils and ills of the world, to rid our conscious minds, if even for a short time, of the news of the day.

Storyteller, Kristin Olson-Huddle,[4] whose parents were both killed in an accident when she was a child, tells the story of her favorite aunt, Gale, who comforted her:

"So we snuck upstairs, away from the rest of the family to my cousin's bedroom. She had her bed up on posts. Gale and I sat together under the bed. We sat with knees touching, holding hands."

> Gale: "Am I here?"
>
> Kristin: "Yeah."
>
> Gale: "How do you know?"
>
> Kristin: "I can see you."
>
> Gale: "Close your eyes. Am I still here?"
>
> Kristin: "Yeah."
>
> Gale: "How do you know?"
>
> Kristin: "I can feel you."

"So she let go of my hands, and scooted back."

> Gale: "Am I here?"
>
> Kristin: "Yeah."
>
> Gale: "How do you know?"
>
> Kristin: "I can hear you."

Gale: (Whispering) "Am I still here?"

Kristin: " … Yeah."

Gale: "How do you know I am here even when you cannot hear me?"

Pause.

Kristin: "I just know."

Gale: "Exactly, just like you know that your parents are still with you."

Our imagination, like the heart muscle of the soul, seeks to know the unknowable:

- *a belief in the afterlife*
- *a solution to some unexplainable, observed phenomenon*
- *a connection with the divine*

Such longings may tempt us to challenge the world of empirical fact—to poke holes in the wall dividing the real from the unreal, the actual from the symbolic, and the world of science from that of imagination.

In so doing, we may allow the world of image, stories, and sensations to loosen the mortar between the bricks in the walls of separation, giving credence to a broader, fuzzier—though perhaps more satisfying—truth.

If we make a practice of this new perspective then, the wall between the real and unreal may remain permeable. In the best of circumstances, allowing the imagination a longer rein invites an initiation into a world rich in language, symbols, and rhythm, a baptism into the sacred, a kind of ephemeral shadow emerges behind the literal physical presence of a place, a phenomenon, or a life.

The most beautiful and most profound experience is the sensation of the mystical. It is the sower of all true science.[5]
—Albert Einstein

A mythic perspective may be achieved as the mind becomes more receptive to and interested in symbolic representations. For instance, when reading myth, references to an underworld can be interpreted as a commentary on the difficult places or passages in our lives.

A story about a demon, or perhaps the story of a Greek God or Goddess, may provide some small window to see our own predicaments in a new light. Likewise, narratives of our lives and of those around us may take on new meaning when we inform them with ancient experience and wisdom.

Our third eye emerges and becomes a more expansive way of looking at our life, our relationships, and our destiny. We are able to negotiate a sideways entry point into eternity that seeks to hold the experience of immortality in a heartbeat, daring to suggest that eternity is not linear, but like truth, it is everywhere in every moment.

The full-color world of metaphor and spirituality takes up residence in our consciousness, our soul, and in our artist life.

One might say that the third eye opens our consciousness to a new, dew-fresh, and satin awareness: the grass smells greener, we have a bit more purpose in our steps as we feel the earth beneath us, we fall in love more easily, and maybe have more compassion for others as we more clearly hear their stories, imagine the hardships of their journeys, and see other human beings as part of our story. Even discordant situations or difficult people may take on new meaning when seen through the lens of a more hopeful perspective which has been expanded by entertaining mythic truths and insights.

Dare we hope that war, and other cruel delusions of separateness, might become a casualty of the life of the imagination?

Hatred is a failure of the imagination.
— Graham Greene, *The Power and The Glory*

> "The final years have a very important purpose:
> The fulfillment and confirmation of one's character.
> When we open our imaginations to the idea of the ancestor,
> aging can free us from convention
> and transform us into a force of nature,
> releasing our deepest beliefs for the benefit of society."
> —James Hillman, *The Force Of Character*

Chapter 5

Signal Trees[1]

Elders and Mentors

We may feel alone during our lives, especially during crisis and new challenges. However, there are almost always mentors willing to help if we are open to them: friends and family, professional counselors, clerics, and healers. When Robinson Crusoe saw a footprint in the sand and realized he was not alone, that made all the difference. We are almost never truly alone, although in the most difficult times, we feel as if we are. Like Crusoe, we need to notice the footprints in the sand. Our parish priest once mentioned Robinson Carusoe's moment of hope in a eulogy for a young cousin of mine who had been murdered.

The priest paused after the reference, looked into the eyes of the parents, then said,

Look around you; the footprints are everywhere.

Elders, particularly, can be wellsprings of wisdom, compassion, and support to help us along the way. When I have encountered these folks I have tried to listen and to be grateful for what each one had to teach me.

In this section I pay tribute to some of my mentors and their stories.

Pilgrimage to Beech Mountain—America's Storytelling Royalty[2]

Our job on that cool October morning in the early 1980's, was to drive from Jonesborough, Tennessee, up to Banner Elk, North Carolina. I had jumped at the chance to meet the great Appalachian storyteller, Ray Hicks and his wife, Rosa.

My wife, Nan, and I were to deliver the tradition bearer/national treasure, and his wife, safe and sound, to the National Storytelling Festival in Jonesborough, Tennessee.

Along the winding road that drew us up toward Ray and Rosa's place, the farms and fenced fields were perched on melon-like hills, framed by forested ridges and rail fences. The boulder-dotted meadows resembled the drawings I had seen in Richard Chase's *Jack Tales* and *Grandfather Stories*, classic volumes of Appalachian folk tales. I knew that most of the tales that filled those volumes were collected right here on these ridges as part of the Writers Project during the Great Depression.

When I reached Old Mountain Road, below which Ray's unpainted, wood-frame family home would soon appear, the hair on the back of my neck began to rise as I passed mailboxes at the end of hidden driveways.

In order, they read something like:

Hicks, Harmon, Ward, Harmon, Hicks, Hicks, Harmon, Ward ... the simple mailboxes along this country road recited a litany of the most historic family names in the annals of Appalachian folklore and storytelling.

These families had continued the oral tradition of telling ancient stories down through the generations—stories that came over from Scotland, Ireland, England, and Germany some two-hundred years ago with ancestors who settled in the Southern Mountains. These mountain folks, who never heard of the Brothers Grimm, Chaucer, or King Arthur, nevertheless told tales from these ancient times. They learned the ancient stories from their grandparents, stories that place Jack of beanstalk fame in bib overalls, chopping wood, eating cat-head biscuits and red-eye gravy, and chasing down unicorns and giants for the king—or any rich landowner, since there never have been kings in North America.

Ray Hicks often said that:

Whenever there was some slow work like huskin' corn, or some such thing, I'd keep the young'uns workin' by tellin' 'em about Jack. Why they wouldn't say a word ... just kept at it as long as I was tellin' 'em tales.[3]

Years later, on a visit, I helped Ted Hicks, Ray and Rosa's son, load cinder block for an addition onto their house. They had no running water up until that time. This new cinder block would be the foundation for a modern bathroom.

Ted was ill that day but he could drive the pickup truck back and forth from the cinder block pile to the building site. While I loaded, he leaned against the pickup bed and told one story after another, some about Jack, some, like the "Miller's Wife," that scholars date back to Chaucer's Canterbury Tales. I guess Ted had listened well and shucked a lot of corn.

My wife and I parked on a gravel turnout twenty feet or so above the house, which seemed to sit on the shoulder of the ridge. The porch was neatly stacked with firewood—each piece sorted and stacked by size, right down to the starter twigs which were sticks shaved with whittled, curled edges.

Corn stood, dry-stalked and yellow, in the side yard. We passed a springhouse and hand pump as we walked toward the front porch. We knew we were being granted an audience with an oracle. That I would walk that path many times in the next twenty years or so was beyond my wildest hopes.

Ray came out onto the porch to meet us—all six-foot seven-inches of him; he looked tall and narrow as a pine sapling. Rosa, at least a foot and a half shorter, stood alongside of him and gave us a "howdy" and a warm smile.

They invited us to the house to sit while Rosa gathered some items to sell at the festival: huckleberry turnovers, angelica root, carvings that their son, Ted, had made, and some herbs, folk medicines, and crafts.

While Rosa was loading some small cardboard boxes, Ray sat

down in his easy chair next to the wood burning stove, and started telling us a story about Jack. I don't remember if we had asked him for a story or not, but we were certainly grateful to hear one.

As Ray told the story, we could hear Ted laughing in a dark corner, listening intently to the familiar stories, and occasionally spitting his Beech Nut tobacco juice into a coffee can.

When Ray and Rosa were ready to leave, I asked Ted if he would like to go down to the National Festival with his folks.

No, I believe I'll stay right here.

Ted Hicks played the traditional role of the son who stayed home to care for his parents and welcome strangers.

Ted was shy. It would be years before he'd set foot on the National Storytelling Festival stage, charged with filling his father's shoes as the master storyteller of the family. Ted had learned the stories in the time-honored tradition, surrounded by family and neighbors.

With Rosa all packed, we headed out the door. Ray continued the storytelling as we walked up the path to our car, as we drove down the mountain, and finally, all the way into Jonesborough. He told these stories (false teeth in), interrupted by brief licks on his harmonica (false teeth out).

Once, in between stories, he said,

I hope they give me more than an hour at the Festival this year. Ya can't do much tellin' in an hour.

In fact, we picked Ray and Rosa up at about 10:00 a.m. on that Saturday morning. He told stories all the way to the festival, to reporters and well-wishers who gathered as we walked through the crowds, and during his two, fifty-five minute sets in the festival tents, each with a thousand or so folks in attendance. Then, he told more stories to reporters and fans after each performance.

Ray kept on telling and singing as we drove back up the mountain, and all during Rosa's dinner of hot biscuits, apple sauce, country ham and home-canned beans, topped off with black-berry pie—all prepared on her wood-burning cook stove.

After approximately fourteen hours of non-stop storytelling, Ray followed Nan and me up the path ... telling us stories all the way to the car and through the open passenger window as we started back down the gravel mountain road.

Ray, Rosa, and Ted are all gone now, though their stories still echo in those mountains and far beyond. I talked on the phone to Ted's brother, Lenard, a while back. He said to drop in anytime. I think I will.

I've heard Lenard knows the stores, too.

Duncan Williamson—The Man With Three Thousand Stories

Duncan Williamson—possibly the most extraordinary tradition bearer of the whole Traveller tribe.
—Hamish Henderson, School of Scottish Studies, University of Edinburgh,
writing in A Thorn in the King's Foot: Folktales of the Scottish Travelling People

The Travelling People of Scotland have been nomads for centuries. To this day they travel throughout Scotland producing crafts, performing day labor, and working in the agricultural harvest, among other varied occupations.... The Travellers are also known for their piping, storytelling, and balladeering.

Duncan Williamson, of all his Traveller family, absorbed virtually every story and ballad that he heard in his travels and in the intergenerational encampments where his kin spent winters year after year. Duncan claimed to know three thousand stories and ballads.

No one knows the exact number for sure, but the archive of the School of Scottish Studies at Edinburgh University, houses some fifteen hundred of his narratives. And there are now many published collections of his stories and life's journey, two of the most notable being *The Thorn In The Kings Foot*, and *The Horsieman, Memories of a Traveller 1928-1958*.

According to Duncan's second wife (Duncan's first wife, Jeannie Townsley, died in 1971), scholar and author, Linda Williamson:

> *In the mid-1980's the non-traveller world came*
> *to realize that the oral traditions of the Travelling*
> *People of Scotland were not only a source of valuable*
> *knowledge, but a stronghold of education, probably*
> *unequaled anywhere in Europe. A stream of folk from*

every continent on the earth started to flow into the
[our] *fireside ceilidh* … [(kālē)—a social event at
which there is Scottish or Irish folk music and
singing, traditional dancing, and storytelling.]
—Linda Williamson, from *The Horsieman, Memories of a Traveller
1928-1958.* Edinburgh: Birlinn Limited, 1994.

**I was reared, born, and bred on stories.
That's all I had in my life.**
—Duncan Williamson

Duncan said that he knew his father's stories were something
that would stand him his whole life.

**Even if we had no food to eat, we were full of love for our
father's voice.**
—*Fireside Tales of the Traveller Children* (1983)

Duncan Williamson and I were both featured tellers at the
National Storytelling Festival in 1987. He invited all ten thousand in the audience to come visit him in Scotland. I took him
up on it on several occasions. We became friends. I invited
Duncan to come tell at the Illinois Storytelling Festival, as well
as to visit in our home.

At The National Festival, Duncan met Ray Hicks, the preemi-
nent tradition bearer of Appalachian Jack Tales. Duncan, who
claimed to know some sixty stories about Jack, of Scottish origin,
was struck by the appearance of the tall, lean mountain man. At
one of the sessions that we shared, I remember Duncan telling
the audience …

**I've always wondered what Jack looked like,
and now, seeing Ray Hicks, I know."**

Two years later, in 1989, I first visited Duncan in his cottage in Auchtermuchty, Fife, Scotland, where he lived with his wife, Linda, and their children, Tommy and Betsy.

We sat up together on that first night, next to a roaring coal fire. Duncan told me one story after another, the wind outside like salt for the tales. Duncan put as much into telling a story to one person as he would to a full room or auditorium, or in the case of our National Festival, a thousand people or more.

Duncan looked you right in the eye. Sometimes kneeling at your feet at a particularly dramatic point in the story—a likely vestige of his Traveller days when he lived in tents, telling and listening to stories while sitting, kneeling, or lying on the ground.

The summer mornings come early in Scotland. Once, before Duncan got up, I had taken a walk along a narrow roadside. Wood pigeons flew overhead, looping along in a bright, blue, high sky.

I watched a silver fox tiptoe along a hand built dry wall, the kind that Duncan said he built in earlier days—one of the many trades that provided a living during his years on the road before he settled in as, perhaps, the greatest traditional storyteller in the English, Scottish, and Cant (Traveller dialect) languages.

Back at his cottage, Duncan leaned across his teacup.

Jim, did you ever hear about the time that Jack went to school?

Well, I had not. There was no mention of Jack going to school in Richard Chase's classic Jack Tales. Nor had I ever heard Ray Hicks talk about Jack going to school. So I thought to myself that:

Here I am, sitting in a cottage in Scotland, ready to hear a story from one of the greatest ... a story which, as far as I knew, had never been written down.

" No, Duncan. I've never heard about Jack going to school."

"Jack went to school for the first time when he was eighty years old, Jim, Would you like to hear about it?"

"Yes, Duncan, I certainly would!"

Jack Goes to School *(A Scottish Jack Tale)*

I sat that morning, ready and eager, for this rare story that perhaps had never been written down but rather was part of Duncan's vast remembered repertoire. As Duncan re-filled our teacups before beginning his story, I remembered reading some scholars' claim that a deep well of unknown traditional stories had been discovered thanks to Duncan and his Traveller family.

Duncan began:

> Like always, Jack was poor. Why, he didn't hardly have anything to eat but 'taddies' (potatoes). He was an old man living with his daughter and granddaughters. Jack worked hard in the garden every day, even though he was 80 years old.

> He raised just enough 'taddies' to feed his daughter and granddaughters, to sell a few to the fisherman and small crofters (farmers) nearby, and to provide peelings for the chickens.

> Times were hard for Jack's family and for his neighbors. If they ever did make a little money the king's men would hear about it and find a way to tax

them out of it, or steal it outright.

Well, one day Jack was in the garden pulling weeds and picking potato bugs when he heard a rumbling on the roadway, the creaking of harness, and the crack of a whip. Jack looked up and there came a fine carriage, black and shiny with sparkling bronze lanterns glinting in the sun. Two powerful white horses in a silver-trimmed harness pulled the carriage.

The horses were at a dead gallop, thundering down the road toward Jack's cottage, their ears pinned back, humping at a ferocious clip they were. [Duncan's eyes lit up; he was an accomplished horsetrader.]

That must be someone important in such a carriage, thought Jack. Maybe even the king or one of his court ministers.

As the carriage passed Jack, it hit a hole in the road. The coach jostled, causing an iron chest to fall out the back. The horses never broke stride as the carriage disappeared in a dusty cloud.

"Now, Jim, wouldn't you be curious about that chest?"—Duncan looked at me as if this event had just happened in front of his cottage.

Well, there never was anyone more curious than Jack. So he walked over and pried open the box."

It was filled with shiny, gold coins.

At this point in the story, Duncan set his teacup down, looked at me across the table, his intense blue eyes barely hiding a wink.

Now Jim, Jack would never do a dishonest thing. But, he buried that box six feet in the ground right behind the 'taddie' patch.

Duncan's eyes twinkled.

That night, at supper, Jack told his granddaughters that their grandpa was going to go to school with them in the morning. It would be the first time that Jack had ever stepped foot in a school.

At school the children laughed at Jack, such an old man with skinny, bowed legs! But soon Jack won them over for he knew all the stories, jokes, and riddles.

One of Jack's riddles asked:

What's better than God; worse than the devil; dead men eat it; if you eat it you die?

No one knew

"Nothing," said Jack, "Nothing's better than God, nothing's worse than the devil, dead men eat nothing, and if you eat nothing you die."

The children shrieked with delight and satisfaction; even the teacher enjoyed Jack's stories and riddles. That night at supper his granddaughters asked Jack what he was going to teach them all in school tomorrow?

"I'm quitting school," said Jack. "One day is enough!"

Well, when grandpa spoke, that was the end of it. Jack was done with school.

Time passed and one day, as Jack worked in his potato patch, he looked up to see that same carriage with those same fine white horses. But this time the horses moved at a slow prance and behind the carriage, as far as Jack could see, was a long column of the king's soldiers.

The entire entourage stopped in front of Jack's house. An officer dismounted, adjusted his sword, and approached Jack.

"'The king has lost a great deal of gold, Jack. Have you seen a chest of gold?"

At this point in the story, with a wry and amused look, Duncan says: "Now Jim, Jack would never tell a lie."

"'Yes," said Jack, "I found a chest of gold."

The officer stiffened; his stance now authoritative. His hand clutched the hilt of his sword.

"Jack, when did you find the chest of gold?" he demanded. Jack became thoughtful, his glance surveying the column of soldiers.

"Yes, I remember," said Jack. "It was the day before I went to school."

The officer flinched.

"'The day before you went to school? How old are you, Jack?"

"I'm eighty years old."

"You're eighty years old and you found the gold on the day before you went to school?"

"That's right!" Jack assured the captain.

"Honest as the day is long." Duncan proclaimed with laughter and cunning in his eyes. Duncan's delight in Jack's trickery was infectious, as he relived his own days of living by his wits.

The captain approached the coach, climbed in and spent a bit of time talking to some important official there. When he emerged the captain walked right up to Jack to deliver his decision:

"Jack, if you found that gold on the day before you went to school and you're eighty years old, then it must not be the king's gold."

The troops and the coach continued on their way. Jack never saw them again, and that, according to Duncan, was how Jack finally became a rich man and took good care of his family.

I last spoke with Duncan on the phone in October, 2007. We were both looking forward to my upcoming visit with him at his home in Scotland. When I arrived there I learned that Duncan had had a stroke. He died on November 8th. I did not see Duncan before his death, but did attend his funeral at a small, stone, country church in Fife, November 12, 2007. His was a Travellers' funeral with the coffin led to the grave by his nephew playing the bagpipes. Duncan always said his father used to play the bagpipes for the seals.

See the appendix of this book for the eloquent and heart-felt eulogy for Duncan, composed by Ben Haggerty and Hugh Lupton, and delivered by Hugh Lupton that day, in the name of the storytelling community—and Jack—I was there; heard it with my own ears.

Jackie Torrence[4] Holds Studs Spellbound

Some thirty years ago I sat in the recording studio of Chicago's

WFMT, 98.7 FM—a radio station known for folk and clas-
sical music—and the ruminations of a Pulitzer Prize-winning
author. Seated across from me were legendary storyteller, Jackie
Torrence, and the revered author, oral historian, labor advocate,
and toast of both Chicago's literati and working class—Studs
Terkel.

We were taping a radio program about storytelling. The program
was to air later on Studs' regular show. Jackie, an African American storyteller, was one of the great forces that moved the storytelling revival forward in the 70's and beyond. She was a self-
made woman, and a single mother. She had gotten interested
in storytelling by telling stories to children at her local library
while working there as a reference librarian. At that time she
never dreamed she would be telling stories at festivals all over
America or be an invited guest on NBC's nationally-syndicated
Late Night with David Letterman.

I had invited her to tell at the Illinois Storytelling Festival in
Spring Grove and Studs was interested in us—especially in
Jackie, and in what this storytelling revival was all about.

At one point during the taping, Jackie, in mid-story, leaned
toward Studs. He leaned back. She was tellin' about Jack, the
trickster and folk hero of the Appalachian and Celtic traditions.
Jackie could modulate her voice, now plaintive and sweet, now
rough and worldly. I sat there thinking, *too bad the radio audience
couldn't watch her amazing eyes,* as she mesmerized Studs.

As usual, Jack and his ma were in a fix. Jackie recounted:

"Why Jack, we're practical starvin' ta death." Jack's ma said.

Studs, riveted, mumbled along with the story, his head nodding up and down.

"If you don't go and seek your fortune, Jack, why we're just not goin' ta make it till spring!"

Studs agreed, shaking his head from side to side, continuing his animated mumbling, and grumbling, as if he were listening to a grave conversation in which he had a stake.

Studs had published numerous collections of oral interviews—the results of thousands of hours of listening to people from all walks of life and in all kinds of life situations but his demeanor suggested that he had never encountered anyone like

the glorious Jackie Torrence in full control of her storytelling powers.

When Jackie and I got back into the elevator after the interview to descend one of Chicago's famous sky-scrapers, we couldn't stop talking about Studs: his humor, his grace and welcoming spirit, his storytelling.

After a while we looked at each other and thought:

This must be an awfully slow elevator ... before realizing that, in our excitement to debrief our time with Studs, we had forgotten to push the lobby button.

Studs Terkel[5]

In my conversations with Studs, whether on his radio show, or on a conference program that we shared, or standing in the popcorn line at a Chicago movie theater, I always found him attentive and present. So I was honored to introduce Studs as the keynote speaker at our National Storytelling Conference in Chicago, some years ago. That day he told the story of being robbed at gunpoint in his apartment one predawn morning. The intruder made Studs give him his wallet and all his cash.

At one point Studs implored the man:

Hey, every morning I go down to the corner and get a paper and a cup of coffee.
How about you give me five bucks back for that?

The thief looked stunned for a moment, and then reached into the stolen wallet and handed Studs a five dollar bill. How's that for being a persuasive communicator in a pinch? Even if you were a thief, stealing his money, you couldn't help but like Studs and want to do him a good turn.

Always a union man, suspicious of big companies, he would tell this story of the thief giving him back the five dollars, then hold his hand up toward the audience as if there was money in it and say:

This five bucks that I got back … It's like the corporate foundation. They steal most of your money and give you back a pittance in the form of a grant.

When I talked to Studs to get some background for my introduction at the conference he had lost most of his hearing.

I'm deaf as a post, he said, but we will have fun with it.

We did have fun, indeed. Just to breathe the same air with Studs was enough. Though I don't think anything can top that moment at the radio taping, watching two of my heroes meeting for the first time. I had witnessed two of the great communicators who owed their success and power to the ability to completely give themselves over to a story.

Inez Ashdown[6] and the Last Queen of Hawai'i

Inez spoke English and Hawaiian. Her voice was a smooth and satiny whisper. She was of Scottish descent, with thick, elegant, snow-white hair. Her fair skin was rough, spotted, and wrinkled, having been sacrificed to the islands' tropical sun, under which she had spent all but a few years of her life. Around her neck, she always wore layers of fresh flower leis brought to her nearly every day as tribute by her frequent admiring visitors. She wore the traditional island missionary *mu'umu'u*.

As a small child, Inez had come to Maui from Wyoming with her cowboy father and her mother. Her father came to work cattle at the vast 'Ulupalakua Ranch on the slopes of the extinct volcano, Haleakalā, on the island of Maui. Her father, a mainland *haole* (white person) had won the US calf roping title. He was hired to work on the cattle ranch with the Hawaiian cowboys, the *paniolos*.

It was the turn of the twentieth century—a time when Hawai'i's last monarch, the much-loved Queen Lili'uokalani, though deposed, was still living among her people. When we met Inez she was eighty-eight years old, and the historian emeritus of Maui County. As a young girl, Inez had known the queen, who would visit 'Ulupalakua Ranch.

A student of mine had told me about Inez and now she had granted my wife, Nan, and me an interview in her small cottage near Kahului, Maui.

"I am a woman of two worlds and two civilizations,"
Inez proclaimed during our first meeting.

Inez reconciled her Catholicism with a deep respect for the ancient Hawaiian religion and way of life. She maintained a passionate devotion to the power of *Pele*, the volcano goddess and mother of the islands, and to the life of a cowgirl. On one visit, she claimed that, in her youth, she would:

... skip Sunday Mass to go roping wild cows
on the volcano beds with my paniolo friends.

On one of our yearly visits to see Inez, she spoke of plans to build a thermal energy plant on the Big Island (Hawai'i), on the slopes of the volcano, *Kīlauea* a site considered sacred by Hawaiian elders. Inez sided with the elders. She considered the project a desecration of the land and a direct insult to Pele.

When we returned the following year, Inez announced with righteous satisfaction that,

"She (Pele) *showed them*" by blowing the site of the proposed thermal energy plant to smithereens with her latest eruption!

The new activity of the volcano had completely thwarted the controversial project.

One afternoon, Inez began talking about Queen Lili'uokalani. Inez thought the queen a virtual saint who embodied Hawai'i's Aloha Spirit of love and harmony. When she spoke about the queen, Inez's broad smile would send her sun lines, spots, and scars scattering across her face.

Inez told us that, as a youth, she had attended the private school, Punahou. Since she lived on Maui, Inez took correspondence classes and traveled by steamer to the Island of O'ahu to take exams in person at the school. On one of these occasions, the queen was driving up the Mānoa Valley in a carriage when she spotted Inez walking to school.

"She knew me because we would visit when she came to the 'Ulupalakua Ranch," Inez explained.

**"Inez, ride with me, I will take you up the valley,"
offered the queen.**

As Queen Lili'uokalani and Inez rode up the Mānoa Valley toward Punahou Springs, the queen told Inez the story of twin orphans abandoned by the springs. Their parents gone, the children were in danger of starving. The twins were taken under the care and protection of *Kākea the Mo'o*, a water spirit that can take the form of a dragon or a lizard. In Hawaiian myths, some Mo'o are benevolent and do much good.

Kākea showed the twins where to find food: breadfruit, coconut, and taro. He helped them find the freshest, tastiest spring water. Under his care, the Twins of Punahou Springs prospered and found happiness and contentment, despite the loss of their parents.

The story ended just as Inez and the queen reached the top of the valley. As Inez stepped from the carriage, the queen said,

"'Okay, Inez, you go study now and do good on your tests.'"

Inez was quiet after telling the story. It seemed to take her some time to leave behind the memory of that magical ride with the last queen of Hawai'i. Then, Inez's face seemed to soften as she once again drank in the meaning of this story for her own life.

The queen was such a wonderful woman. I think she told me that story because she knew that papa and mama were getting a divorce, that mama was returning to Wyoming, and that I would be staying on Maui with my father, my horses, and nā paniolo.

The queen wanted me to know that, in Hawai'i, the children were always taken care of.

The Hawaiian orphan-gods of which Queen Lili'uokalani spoke were twins. The boy-child was named Ka ua wa 'ahila (meaning the rain of Wa'ahila) and the girl was named Ka ua ki'owao (meaning the cool mountain mist or rain).

To this day, the spirits of the two children (the rain and the mist) can be seen in the upper valley where they took refuge.

Carl and Helen—Building an Elders' Circle

I co-founded the Illinois Storytelling Festival (ISF), and was its artistic director for twenty years. During that time, ISF invited elders who had led interesting lives to come tell their stories. My friend and colleague, storyteller Michael Cotter, who is a third-generation farmer from Minnesota, and I, led workshops for elders as a festival outreach program sponsored by The Illinois Department On Aging, a state agency.

At that time, Mike and I were crafting many of the stories we were telling from our own experiences and from the tales we heard growing up in our families and hometowns.

After several of these meetings, it was time for Mike and me to be quiet, time to let the elders speak. We were not sure what might happen.

I remember our first participator meeting:

Carl and Helen sat to my right in a rough circle made by library tables and chairs. They had been regular attendees at The Illinois Storytelling Festival and at these workshops that Michael and I were conducting. I turned to Carl and asked him:

"Carl, do you have a story to tell?"

A D-Day Story

Carl, a slight man, wiry, in his seventies, didn't speak at first. The room grew quiet.

Then he said, "I was at Omaha Beach on D-Day."

The silence in the room deepened.

> I was in the second landing group. The first group went in at 7:00 o'clock and we were supposed to go in at 8:00 o'clock, but we went in at 7:30 because that first group didn't do so good. Some guys couldn't swim. When the landing craft stopped in deep water they sunk with their heavy packs and drowned.
>
> Those of us who got to the beach just kept on moving. I don't know how I made it. You'd look beside you and your buddy would be there. Then

you'd look again and he would be gone. Some guys would just be torn apart. But you just had to keep goin'.

The rest of the circle listened in reverential silence.

"I made it through that day in Normandy and then all the way through the Battle of the Bulge—and Africa."

I thanked Carl. Then I looked at his wife, Helen.

Helen's Story

"Helen, do you have a story?"

"Oh no," she said, "I just come to listen with Carl."

Helen was always with Carl. They'd walk into our meetings, sometimes, hand in hand—a loving couple who had been married for a long time.

"Come on, Helen, you must have a story."

"No," she laughed and patted Carl on the head. "I'm just so happy to come with Carl to storytelling; and so grateful that he came back from the war."

I asked her one more time, maybe because I had been a classroom teacher and had a hunch.

"Oh come on, Helen, you must have a story."

The smile left Helen's face. She looked around the group, down at her hands and then back at us as she began to speak.

We had a baby with Down Syndrome ... Patty. At first, I didn't understand. They didn't bring me my baby. I kept asking for my baby. Finally a doctor came in. He was very mean.

He said, "It is a mongoloid; we will institutionalize her for you."

His words were pointed like arrows. It was as if he was blaming me for having given birth to my child. Carl and I didn't know what to do.

Finally, I remember the day that I told the nun at the hospital that we were taking our Patty home. And I remember the nun smiled and said, "Good."

We just didn't know what to do. I picked up a book about Down Syndrome and would cry every time I read it. Finally, Carl took the book away from me. He said,

We're not going to read the book anymore. We are just going to take it a little at a time.

Carl had been to the war and he knew that you just have to take things a step at a time.

Then Helen became very quiet. She looked around the room at each of us.

I want you all to know how much love that child, our Patty, brought into our marriage.

And we all knew. We had seen the proof every time the two of them walked into the room.

Chapter 6

Toxic Paths and Transformation

A Long, Crooked Path to Redemption

According to the story, the Baal Shem Tov, the legendary mystical rabbi and founder of the Hassidic[1] sect of Judaism, had gathered his disciples around his deathbed. He looked up at each disciple and gave each a task that he hoped would keep his teachings alive.

The Baal Shem Tov charged a particular disciple with the task of traveling throughout Europe telling the stories that the master had taught. This task would be a lifelong commitment, cautioned the master, but there would be some time in the future, unknown at the present, when this disciple could rest.

Some say that the disciple had wished for something better than the life of a penniless, itinerant storyteller. However, out of his great respect and devotion to the Baal Shem Tov, he obeyed. For many years, he traveled the length and breadth of Eastern and Western Europe, telling stories—spreading the Judaic teachings as they were so beautifully expounded by his master.

Many years followed, each year filled with travel, hardships, and sometimes an empty stomach. Yet, the humble disciple persevered in his arduous, yet holy task.

Finally, late in life, the storyteller received a request to travel to Spain where a certain wealthy merchant had requested his presence. This important man wished to hear the stories of the great Baal Shem Tov. The disciple took up the journey to Spain with some anticipation. Perhaps, he thought, this was the fulfillment of the master's prediction that someday there would be rest, and that his itinerant life would end.

Upon arriving at the residence of the wealthy man, the disciple was greeted warmly by the servants who knew of their employer's desire to hear The Baal Shem Tov's stories.

After a fine dinner, he was taken to a bedroom where tapestries and silks hung from the walls. Here he retired for the evening. In the morning he was to meet his host and tell the wonderful stories.

The next day, the storyteller was led into a library where his host waited to hear the stories. The wealthy patron of the arts and of all things holy in that city rose when the disciple entered the room.

"Come, come my friend. Please be seated. I am so very grateful that you have traveled this long journey to bring the Baal Shem Tov's stories to me."

The gracious host motioned to an ebony chair, inset with fine ivory, in which a silken cushion offered elegance and comfort.

The storyteller lowered himself into the chair, adjusted his position a bit and prepared to speak. But alas, for the next several moments there was nothing but silence in the room. Try as he might, the Baal Shem Tov's disciple could not remember a single story.

Finally, the kind man leaned toward the storyteller and assured him that the traveling must have worn him out, and insisted that he should rest. They would try again in the morning.

But day after day, this futile and, for the storyteller, humiliating exercise was repeated with not a story to be remembered.

Finally, the sympathetic merchant presented the Baal Shem Tov's disciple with a small bag of coins for his trouble and dismissed him. But as the storyteller was leaving the library, he hesitated at the door.

"Dear Sir, I have just remembered one short story. It seems like very little but at least I could leave you with one story, however insignificant."

Yes, of course, The merchant brightened a bit, and invited the disciple back to his chair.

The storyteller began,

> The master and all of his disciples were gathered during the Christian Holy Week before Easter. We did not travel during this week because of the danger. All over Eastern Europe Jews were attacked and harassed during this time, accused of killing Christ and of other hateful lies.

> The Baal Shem Tov approached me and told me to prepare a horse and carriage so that he and I could travel to a nearby city for an appointment. I was terrified to go out in public. But for my deep faith in the Master's vision and my loyalty to him I would

not have been able to do as I was told.

Somehow we traveled safely to the city. We wound our way through back alleys until we arrived at the backdoor of a house which fronted the city plaza. As I tied the horse, the back door opened and several men and women greeted the Master as if they were old friends.

We had some soup and wine and rested for a short time.

I had noticed that heavy curtains were drawn over the windows to the street. Responding to my inquiries, the head of the household told me that there would be a solemn Christian procession that day in observance of the death and resurrection of Christ.

The bishop himself would be taking part and that it would be very dangerous for any Jew to be seen. It was not unusual for a Jew to be seized and executed by a crowd amid chants of,

"Christ-killer."

Soon we heard a rhythmic drumbeat and the voices of a large crowd reciting prayers in unison. At that moment the Baal Shem Tov asked me to go out into the street and inform the bishop that he, the Baal Shem Tov, wished to speak with his Excellency!

I was horrified. I knew it would be the last day of my life. But I obeyed my master and opened the door onto the street. Hundreds of worshippers sang as they processed. There was the slow beating of a drum and the mournful sound of brass instruments. Incense filled the air. Young boys carried crosses on tall poles and men carried gold-tasseled banners with images of the Crucifixion.

Behind the banners, marching acolytes were swinging smoking censors. Then came a team of prancing black horses drawing an ornate carriage. The bishop stood in the back of the carriage, dressed in a black cassock and wearing a mitre on his head. He held a golden staff in one hand as he turned from side to side blessing the crowd. His two fingers were raised, making the sign of the cross, delicately bestowing holy benediction as he mumbled the proper prayer for the occasion.

And then he whispered something to his driver and the carriage stopped.

To my surprise, the bishop called for me to come up alongside the carriage. He bent low and asked if I knew the Baal Shem Tov. I told the bishop that I was one of his disciples. He nodded as if he suspected as much. And then, in a moment that I will never forget, I watched the bishop descend from his high place on the grand coach. The bishop then asked me to take him to my master.

I lead the bishop to the home where we had all gathered. The Baal Shem Tov and the bishop greeted each other and then adjourned to an adjacent room where they conferred for some time behind a locked door. In the outer room, everyone fidgeted and murmured among themselves.

After awhile we heard the crowd outside beginning to chant the bishop's name. There came a heavy fist striking the door. Just then the bishop and the Baal Shem Tov emerged from the room. They embraced and the bishop left. The crowd cheered him as he resumed his prominent seat in the Holy Week procession.

The Baal Shem Tov turned to me and asked that I prepare our carriage since our work was accomplished.

And that is all I can recall. I know it is not much of a story.

The disciple stared at the floor for some moments. He was certain that his host would be disappointed with such an uneventful and seemingly meaningless story. Finally, the disciple managed the courage to face the eyes of the rich man and found that his host was slumped forward in his chair, his head in his hands, quietly sobbing. When the kind merchant had composed himself he said:

> I remember you well, now. I was there that day.
> I was that bishop of whom you spoke. I am a Jew
> but at that time, under a terrible, harsh wave of
> persecution, I renounced the faith of my birth and
> became a Christian.

> I am a man who understands the reins of power and
> so I was able to ascend to the office of bishop. I kept
> my true beliefs secret. I am deeply ashamed that
> I even participated in the annual execution of the
> archetypal Jew during Holy Week.

> The night before the Easter procession of which you
> spoke, I had a terrible dream that my soul was lost.

> Now, I had secretly followed the teachings of
> the Baal Shem Tov, so during the procession I
> recognized you as one of his followers. Still troubled
> by my dream, I asked to see your master.

> We spoke for a long time. He told me that my soul
> was in grave danger. But there was hope for my
> salvation. He said that I should resign my position
> as the Christian bishop, give up my properties and
> move to a distant land to do good works and help
> the poor.

> All this I have done.

"The great Baal Shem Tov"—here the wealthy man's words choked off as he wept again—"told me that I would know that my soul could rest, that I was forgiven, when someone came to tell me my own story."

The merchant invited the Baal Shem Tov's disciple to remain as a guest in comfort and dignity for the rest of his days to continue his storytelling and teaching.

Refusing to forgive is like trying to kill another by drinking poison yourself.
—Anonymous

Gandhi's Outrageous WWII Proposal

A journalist asked Mahatma Gandhi if he would have attempted non-violent civil disobedience against Hitler in World War II.

The peacemaker replied that he would have done so.

When the startled journalist exclaimed that such a policy would have caused a terrible loss of life.

The great peacemaker countered that there had been astronomical loss of life with violent resistance to Germany.[2]

Gandhi chose a unique and uncommon path to conflict—peaceful non-resistance. He vigorously disapproved of cowardice. He sought warriors, brave men and women who were willing to die but not kill, for a just cause.

In war after war, nations and their people deceive themselves that war will somehow be worth the horror, loss of life, and the terrible suffering of civilians and soldiers, but these same toxic paths are worn smooth by bloody feet, by millions of soldiers and refugees, over and over again.

The nations of the world continue to relive our sad history of violence, seemingly unaware that the same wrong turns bring on repeated bouts of misery and suffering. Gandhi warned that a nation's use of war—planned violence on a large scale—predictably results in mutual suffering, death, and maiming, as well as unseen damage to survivors.

Duty Calls

Frederick and his family lived in the Trier region of Germany. He and his father and younger brothers milked their dairy cows twice a day. The rest of the time they harvested hay and grain, pulled calves, and raised young heifers. It was this breeding, birthing, and milking of the dairy herd that constituted the heartbeat of the dairy farm, as well as Frederick's passion.

He found that feeding and caring for these vulnerable, curly-headed calves, bursting with new life and friskiness, was not a chore at all but work that anchored him into the rhythms of land and animals. It made him proud to be a farmer.

He didn't know much about Hitler. He hoped there would not be a war. His mother would cry at night for her three brothers who died in World War I. The family's hired man still coughed blood from exposure to mustard gas.

Frederick's father grew wheat to make bread for the troops during the War to End All Wars so he did not have to fight.

Frederick had three loves. First and foremost was his beloved Regina who he longed to marry. Regina's stern father demanded that Frederick make something of himself and save enough money before he and Regina would be allowed to wed.

Then there were the milk cows—heavy, friendly, and smelling of sweet summer grass as they lumbered into their stanchions each morning and night. It was hard work, but for Frederick, the warm, silky milk that the farm sent to the cities would someday pay for a wedding and a stake for Regina and the many children they hoped to have.

Someday, Frederick thought, he would teach his children how to herd the cows on clover-scented, dewy mornings, and how to pull a breeched calf. He would pass on all he had learned.

His third love was the new tractor. Though his father still preferred to work the team of round, powerful, Belgian draft horses, Frederick was proud that his father had agreed to purchase the first tractor in their region, not long after the International Harvester plant began production in 1937.

Frederick loved the International Harvester Model F-12-G with its loud motor under the steel hood. The roar of the engine, the smell of the gasoline and exhaust pleased him. Frederick was small, but athletic, and he had a knack for handling anything mechanical. So much so that the local tractor dealer would bring prospective buyers out to the farm to watch Frederick demonstrate what the big, smoke-belching machine could do.

~~

Then Hitler invaded Poland. War was declared and everything changed. Frederick was drafted and reported by rail to the induction center.

Frederick held Regina in his arms at the train station. Regina's tears soaked his shirt and the cloth napkin which held the dinner rolls and sausage that his mother had wrapped.

During his training, he missed the land and the cows, the kitchen smells, and his mother's clanging of pots and pans, almost as much as he missed Regina.

His one consolation: he trained to drive a panzer tank in the armored division. His prowess with machines had been noticed and he learned quickly. The German Panzer was a work of magnificent mechanical engineering. He loved the speed, the maneuverability—and, of course, it had many times the horsepower of his tractor.

Frederick's panzer division was sent to the Belgian front. He drove his tank along with scores of other panzers across the Belgian border, roaring through the countryside in Hitler's Blitzkrieg.

The first day of the assault, he raised himself up through the hatch for a briefing. His heart sank as he saw the fine fields of flax and of wheat that had been destroyed by the advance of his panzer division. But this is war, he thought, the grain will grow back; still Frederick felt a sense of uneasy wonder at the destructive power of this iron machine.

He looked to his left and right at the identical panzers trailing dust as their clattering broke the silence of the calm, sunny, spring day. He resumed his operating position inside his tank.

Then an artillery shell landed close. An explosion rattled the big tank. Frederick's stomach knotted. The radio crackled. He heard the screams of the tank operator on his flank. Then the radio went silent as the panzer alongside Frederick's burst into flames, having taken a direct hit to its fuel tank.

Frederick pivoted the gun turret and fired round after round in the direction of the coordinates ordered by his commander.

Soon the resistance stopped. Frederick was ordered to cease firing. Opening his hatch and standing up he saw the mangled bodies of the Belgian artillery unit that the panzers had destroyed. The knot in his stomach tightened. This is war, he thought, as he wrestled with the images that he viewed—bloodied bodies strewn in trenches dug into the fields of grain.

Then an order came to close the hatches and to continue to fire, to continue to roll, over fields, through farms, destroying barns and sheds. About the time that his warrior's resolve would wane, another panzer would explode and Frederick would become even more determined to destroy anything that might harm him and his comrades in arms.

Panzers roared through Belgium and into France. Resistance ceased. The tanks rolled on. Frederick stood up in the open hatch and looked around: civilians and French troops, their faces distorted with terror, lay huddled in the ditches, alongside hedges and in every hollow beside the road. There were refugee columns and carts abandoned by their owners who had fled in panic into the fields.[3]

The stiffened bodies of Belgian artillery draft horses lay along the road. Frederick thought of his father's gentle workhorses, Maude and Buttermilk, practically members of the family.

The tanks rolled on and on.

Frederick died in 1944 at the Battle of the Bulge. An American GI had climbed the back of Frederick's tank, pried opened the hatch, and pointed his flame thrower inches from Frederick's face. The GI hesitated a moment, caught off guard by the terror in Frederick's eyes, and then pulled the trigger release.

The American GI received the bronze star for courageously rushing Frederick's tank and thus saving his buddies in the machine gun nest that Frederick had targeted.

When the war ended the American soldier received a hero's welcome and hometown parade in rural Wisconsin, where he had returned to his parents' farm.

Choosing a Crooked Path

The second, alternative story, presents a hypothetical scenario whereby Gandhi's non-violent opposition would have been used in the WWII combat theater; how might a soldier like Frederick have responded?

... Then orders came to prepare for a possible attack. Frederick opened the throttle, muffled noise and vibration filled the cramped space. Then came an indistinct *thump*, and then another *thump, thump*. Thinking there was a break in the tank's track Frederick stopped the tank and opened the hatch. He stretched himself up into the blue sky and spring sunshine.

There, stretched before the tanks, were hundreds of young, Belgian farmers in overalls. They lay on the ground willing to die, but not to kill for their country. They lay in rows as far as the eye could see in the direct path of the panzers, the core of Belgium's youth, many of them farmers just like Frederick.

Looking behind him, he saw the bodies of the young men that he, Frederick, and his grand machine, had crushed. Some were still moaning; others eerily silent, lying still next to puddles of blood that soaked into the loamy cropland.

Most of these bodies were dressed in work clothes, much the same as Frederick would have worn at milking time.

From his radio, came the voice of his commanding officer, ordering the panzer division to continue, to move forward into the sea of prostrated bodies. Frederick sat back down at the controls, his hands shaking; he engaged the clutch, the rumbling, bug-like, steel crawler moved ahead: *thump ... thump ... thump!*

Tears streamed down Frederick's cheeks, he began to vomit. These farmers were of no threat to him. How could his commander, also a farmer, give such orders? He longed for home, for Regina, for his farm, for the calves, and for his tractor.

That night, he climbed out of his tank and disappeared into the woods. He would not fight this fight. He would leave the killing and return to Regina. Somewhere, somehow, he hoped to find them a place.

If the terrible sacrifice by these Belgian youths, the non-violent—though powerful—resistance described here in this story had been widespread, could the German army have maintained its Warrior myth (that these are not human beings that I am killing)? Furthermore, isn't it true that non-violent resistance renders moot the ethic of kill or be killed?

~~~

Soldier's Heart—We Ought to Be Able ...

The great Apache warrior, Geronimo,[4] died in a military prison at Fort Sill, in Lawton, Oklahoma. My friend and storytelling colleague, Elizabeth Ellis, tells of considering a visit to the historical site there while she was driving home to Dallas.

But then she remembered a legend that tells of Geronimo's pacing back and forth in his cell so that he wore a rut in the jail floor.

She also recalled what she knew of Geronimo's life. Two of his wives, his mother, and several children had been killed by Mexican soldiers. His family and people had been forcibly removed from their homeland along the Mexico-US border. They were sent to Florida where they suffered and died from sub-tropical diseases and starvation.

Finally, Geronimo was imprisoned at Fort Sill, where he lived out his life.

Haunted by these images of historical atrocities, Elizabeth tells that she continued driving past the Fort Sill exit, not wanting to be reminded of Geronimo's suffering.

Later however, as Elizabeth tells it, she felt shame for she thought:

> **If he had to live it, I ought to be able to look at it.**

This epiphany changed her perspective in a profound way. Elizabeth recounts that the next time she saw a homeless person on the street she remembered her shame of driving past the site of Geronimo's imprisonment. Elizabeth stopped to talk to the homeless man and was eventually able to help the man find a job.

In all matters pertaining to warfare there exists, no doubt, in the human psyche, a strong propensity to turn away from the horrible reality, to deny, on some level, war's day to day misery, in order to go about the act of living.

We may sometimes refer to the suffering that war begets as unimaginable not because we can't imagine such anguish, but because we find it too painful to do so.

And so governments and media, sometimes for their own manipulative reasons, pander to public fears and timidity: for instance, US soldiers' coffins arriving from Iraq and Afghanistan were declared off-limits to the press, and *Life Magazine* censored photos of casualties during WWII.[5]

This control and management of information during wartime raises the question:

> **Doesn't morality require that all citizens fully absorb, in every cell of their conscience, the enormous costs of war to all people of the world?**

In February of 1991, during the final days of the first Gulf War in Iraq, photojournalist Kenneth Jarecke photographed an Iraqi soldier burned alive, his body frozen and charred, gripping the bombed out windshield housing of his army truck, trying to escape the fiery vehicle right up to the very last moment of his life.[6]

The photo was taken on the "Road to Hell," a stretch of highway where 1,400 retreating Iraqi soldiers, trucks, and equipment were stuck in a virtual traffic gridlock as Allied airplanes strafed them over and over again until everything was destroyed, including the Iraqi soldiers.

Jarecke thought his photo might change the way Americans saw the Gulf War, but every magazine and newspaper editor in America declined to publish the photo until well after the Gulf War was declared over.

The Observer, a British publication, and *The Liberator*, a Parisian daily, were the only media outlets to print the photograph when it came across their editorial desks mere days after the event.

There were 1,400 [Iraqi soldiers] in that convoy, and every picture transmitted until that one came, two days after the event, was of debris, bits of equipment. No human involvement in it at all; it could have been a scrap yard.

That was some dreadful censorship.
—Tony McGrath, *The Observer*, picture editor

〜

If pictures tell stories, the story should have a point. So if the point is the utter annihilation of people who were in retreat and all the charred bodies ... if that's your point, then that's true. And so be it.

I mean war is ugly. It's hideous.
—Lee Corkran, Staff Sgt., military photojournalist

To Corkran, who was awarded the Bronze Star for his Gulf War combat photography, pictures like Jarecke's tell important stories about the effects of American and Allied airpower.

... war photography has an ability not just to offend the viewer, but to implicate him or her as well.
—David Carr, *The New York Times* (2003)

An angry 28-year-old Jarecke wrote in *American Photo* in 1991:

If we're big enough to fight a war, we should be big enough to look at it.

━━━

Even the word *casualty*, used to describe the dead and wounded in war, has its semantic roots in denial. The word casualty stems from the word, casual, dating back to the late Middle English meaning a chance, a chance occurrence or without planning or premeditation. The word casualty continues to be used today, in spite of the fact that the explicit purpose of warring factions on all sides is to inflict injury and death upon the other.

━━━

Facing the reality of war will be difficult, requiring us to wade through obfuscating terms such as "peace-keeper missile" and "collateral damage" in order to assimilate the language and ubiquitous images presented by media. Most of all it will require courage.

What resources could we draw upon to find the courage to open our eyes to the reported barbarity that presents itself every day on our newscasts and computer screens?

When I have had to fortify myself to face a hard-edged truth in my own life—such as illness or death in the family, or a conflict with a loved one or with a business associate, I have often looked to certain stories, some of them traditional and timeless, that have often provided me with a perspective and courage to prevail over fear and confusion. Likewise, in my former occupation as a community college counselor, I have found these stories helpful to my students when advising them.

The Legacy of Traditional Stories

The body of myth, fables, folk tales, and spiritual stories from a variety of cultures can be seen as the compendia of the life stories, dreams, and imaginings of billions of people. The best of these stories, those most useful for the survival of the tribe, the community, the society, have been preserved, improved upon, and passed down through the millennia via the oral tradition.

According to mythologist Michael Meade and others, these stories were often told during rituals and were relied upon by ancient peoples during crisis—when they didn't know what else to do, they turned to story.

The stories fired the imagination and offered hope, taught that fears can be faced, demons can be named and deflated, and that brokenness can be healed.

Envision Peace—The Power of Ideas

In our modern era, stories of past successes can fuel our imaginations. Perhaps stories can lead us to new, life-enhancing perspectives and actions, replacing the tired, and ultimately destructive reliance on war to solve international conflicts.

For instance, could a Marshall Plan—US funding for the rebuilding of Germany and Japan after WWII—be implemented in the Middle East, or any impoverished country with a crumbling infrastructure? If the three trillion dollars—US spending on wars in Iraq and Afghanistan—had been spent on hospitals, schools, roads, and bridges, would it be a safer, healthier world today?

Most traditional stories are fundamentally about moral choices, compassion and justice—the building blocks of a well-lived life and perhaps, of a well-ordered, peaceful world.

One such story that addresses the need to confront difficult situations or perhaps even to face-up to the horrors of war is told by Persian poet, Rumi.[7] He recounts the following:

> One dervish to another,
>
> What was your vision of God's presence?
>
> I haven't seen anything. But for the sake of conversation, I'll tell you a story:
>
> God's presence is there in front of me, a fire on the left, a lovely stream on the right. One group walks towards the fire, [then] into the fire, another toward the sweet flowing water.

No one knows which is blessed, and which not.
Whoever walks into the fire appears suddenly in the
stream.

A head goes under on the water surface, that head
pokes out of the fire.

Most people guard against going into the fire,
and so end up in it.

Those who love the water of pleasure [and safety]
and make it their devotion are cheated with this
reversal.

The trickery goes further.
The voice of the fire tells the truth saying,

I am not fire.
I am fountainhead.
Come into me and don't mind the sparks.
—Rumi

A certain warrior spirit, commitment, and resolve, is required to listen to the pain of someone who has been to war. One must enter the fire—listen to their story—with them in order to give comfort.

To stand with a victim of war is to stand with compassion and without judgment.

Currently, soldiers returning from Iraq and Afghanistan with profound emotional pain are frequently diagnosed as having Post Traumatic Stress Disorder (PTSD).[9] During the Civil War, such trauma was called something else.

The Civil War and Soldier's Heart[8]

Soldiers returning from The War Between the States with debilitating emotional wounds were said to have Soldier's Heart

America's 19th-century sensibilities apparently understood that sending young men off to war, to kill or be killed, was likely to break their hearts. A broken heart is generally treated with sympathy and compassionate understanding.

For doesn't it seem likely that if we place young soldiers, some of whom, according to cognitive psychologists, have not fully developed their judgment and reasoning, into the social and moral *disorder* that is war, that it will lead to broken hearts and broken spirits.[9]

So, should we consider that the term Post Traumatic Stress Disorder is *inaccurate* at best, and at worst, that these words are destructive to the dignity of those who have suffered and are trying to heal? Could it be that the labeling of these men and women, the very nomenclature, undermines their hope of recovery? Isn't war itself the disorder into which we send our young people?

The Baal Shem Tov story, in an earlier chapter of this volume, tells of the great Jewish teacher instructing his disciples that *when the bonds between heaven and earth are so utterly threatened, what's needed is more than prayer—what's needed is:*

Words from a broken heart.

If we recognize the reality and truth of the wars that we wage, and, in so doing, walk straight into a kind of fire, can we, perhaps, eventually come to some solace, some healing water that allows us to see the presence of God's wisdom, as Rumi suggests? Or, like the broken-hearted disciple in the Baal Shem Tov story, could we mend the bonds between heaven and earth and heal the wages of war?

And, for our veterans' sake, can we listen to their stories, standing with them side by side, as they speak their broken-hearted words, as they mend their souls and spirits?

Can the citizens of the most powerful country in the world accept the risk—face the fear of walking into the fire of recognition of what our war policies wreak upon the young and old of our world, including our own veterans? Can we walk into that fire on a bet, on a hope, on a peddler's dream? If so, might we someday arrive at the absolving and cleansing pool—the waters of peace?

Finally, if we were to look at the everyday reality of war, is it too much to believe that, armed with a new compassionate rage against the horror and scourge of war, we as citizens of the United States and of the world, could stand against the killing and destruction?

That we could, in one thunderous voice, launch a clarion call that would travel around the world, proclaiming:

ENOUGH IS ENOUGH!

> **Never doubt that a small group of thoughtful committed citizens can change the world; indeed, it's the only thing that ever does.**[10]
> —Margaret Mead

Chapter 7

Trails End and Transformation

My Sister Diane

October 31, 2000, brought a hazy, late autumn day to McHenry County, Illinois. Comparing the seasons of the year to the seasons of a lifetime, these fall days were the best of middle age. The intense, vibrant, procreative, and planting days of spring and summer had passed, and there came a time of quiet beauty. The autumn leaves, though drier and more brittle, had taken on the glorious spectrum of a winter sunset, as if the bright, and glaring, summer sun had aged to deeper, vintage hues.

Sugar Maple leaves whispered their faded red and coral—just a hint of their glory of a few days ago.

The night before, a rain had stripped the cadmium leaves off the Norway Maples, leaving yellow shadows beneath bare, gray boughs bracing for winter.

For the farmers, it was a time of great industry. Semitrailer trucks and farm wagons filled with shelled corn were traveling the country roads and leaving small piles of summer sun spilled at blacktopped intersections, and on sharp curves.

In the fields, mammoth harvesters made great clouds of swirling crushed stalks so that each machine looked as if it were driving through a dust storm.

A smoky, sweet smell of decay hung heavy in the warm, dry air—a reminder that winter loomed to the North. Soon there would be frozen ground, an end to yard work, and rest for the farmers and the land.

It had been a busy Halloween week of telling ghost stories, but now I was done with that genre for a while. I looked forward to working out in the garden, and maybe having some time to put together a new story.

Winter Tales, a storytelling festival in Oklahoma City, had invited me to come tell stories in February. The festival had a tradition in which selected tellers conducted a workshop called *Finding Your Storytelling Voice*. Each storyteller's task was to tell a unique version of the same story—a story that we storytellers had agreed upon in advance, but adapted without consulting one another. The new versions told back to back at the event would be a surprise to the audience as well as to me and my storyteller colleagues. Our group of invited, featured tellers that year agreed upon the story of Noah's Ark.

I had wanted *Dante's Inferno*.

Since I had been raised Roman Catholic in the 50's, before the reforms of the Second Vatican Council, I had spent thousands of hours in my youth digesting images of hellfire so I thought that I could finally cash in on my suffering. However, my Protestant colleagues were having none of it.

I relented. Noah's story had always interested me. There certainly is adequate drama and irony in the story of an unforgiving, wrathful God destroying nearly all of the inhabitants of the world with water. Imagine choosing *water*, the element without which life is impossible.

As I re-read Genesis, I found more irony and even humor. For instance, it came to me that the fish must have been doing something right.

For, if I'm a fish, and I hear the Lord say,

"I will destroy the beasts of the land and the birds of the air with a great flood."

I'm thinking, NO PROBLEM. All this means to me is more worms in the water, and I can swim wherever I want.

And then there was the matter of the carpenters. I had worked summers in the construction trade while in high school, in college, and then as a teacher during my summer vacations. So I had some occasion to work with carpenters. In later years, I had watched them build a beautiful house for our family.

Now, carpenter-speech often contains a certain profane word that, like Noah's story, has to do with what many would call divine intervention, but also with physical creation. The properties of this swear-word are not only dramatic and graphic, but the word can be uttered with amazing utility in a variety of contextual and grammatical syntaxes.

Furthermore, the work situations in which the profanity is

evoked are often accompanied by strong emotion, and expressed to some apprentice or underling on the job, lending even more excitement and color to a rhetorical flourish that might sound like this:

Hey kid, go to that f-ing tool box, and get that f-ing hammer, and get your f-ing butt back here in a f-ing hurry—you little f-er.

Well, when it came right down to it, the carpenters who built Noah's Ark were building an ark to contain two of each type of critter in order to procreate and preserve their species. And since, I would imagine, on that Ark there would be a lot of procreation going on—I'm not sure what else there would be to do, trapped in a smelly boat for forty days and forty nights.

So, those carpenters really were building an f-ing Ark, the term has stuck and the carpenters have been talking that way ever since.

So, I was pleased to have some time off that October thirty-first to study a new perspective on this story of the Great Flood.

That day I had also received an invitation to attend the observance of All Souls Day on November second at my hometown church, Saint Peter's Catholic Church in Spring Grove, Illinois.

All Souls Day is a day Catholics pray for the souls of the dead— *the faithful departed*—who might need additional prayers to enter heaven.

All Souls Day follows All Saints Day, November first, on which the saints in heaven—anybody who has made it into heaven, famous or otherwise, are honored. So it could be St. Joseph himself to whom we'd pray. On the other hand, it might be Walt the calf-buyer, who never missed Mass, was good to his wife and kids, and gave money to the church, that you could honor and say prayers to on All Saints Day.

All Saints and All Souls Days are Christianity's response to pagan feasts like the Celtic Samhain,[1] held at the end of the harvest season.

⌒

As the days shortened and a cool mist moved across the land, ancient people observed All Hallows Eve (October 31), as well as November first and second as a liminal time, a threshold period when the veil between the world of the living and the world of the dead became thin and permeable, with the perceived breaking down of barriers between the material and spirit realms. Communication was thought to become possible between the living and the dead. In Mexico, these harvest feasts and devotions converged on November first and second, with the celebration of Dia de Los Muertos—Day of the Dead. Though an ancient feast, celebrated in the summer by indigenous peoples, it was moved to November to correspond to Spanish Catholicism's All Saints and All Souls Days.

For Catholics, November second has long been a much anticipated, sacred, and cherished time to pray for loved ones who have died. The prayer most often recited on All Souls Day,

May the souls of the faithful departed, through the mercy of God, rest in peace, Amen,

is surely one of the most compassionate in all of Catholic life.

All Saints Day, November first, was a day of celebration and designated as a *Holy Day of Obligation*, on which our Catholic school was closed, and everyone was required to attend Mass.

The priest wore white vestments to signify purity—the state of those whose souls had earned their heavenly reward. We children loved the day. There was no school, and our thoughts dwelt upon those who had escaped hell and were in heaven—meaning we all had at least *a chance* of avoiding eternal damnation.

All Souls Day, on the other hand, was somber. School reopened, but all students were directed by our teaching nuns to arrive at school early enough to attend the morning Requiem Mass for the Dead, before classes.

The priest wore black vestments and dirges droned from the organ in the choir loft as Mass was offered for what we called the poor souls in purgatory. Those were the folks who still suffered in the purifying flames—purging their souls of sin so that they might become worthy to enter heaven.

In the evening, we attended prayers and Benediction in church. After Benediction, a kind of ritual "Amen" to the liturgy of the night, the parishioners lit candles and walked in a procession down the sidewalk, past the Grotto of the Virgin of Fatima, and over the bridge spanning the Nippersink Creek. Then we processed slowly up the hill to Saint Peter's Cemetery where my grandparents, and many of my aunts, and uncles, were buried.

For the children of the parish, on All Souls Night, death seemed to peek around every tombstone. Innocent imaginations shifted from the light-hearted ghouls, zombies, and mummies of trick-or-treating, two nights before, to the considering of dead neighbors rotting in the ground underfoot as we walked, candles in hand, across the graveyard reciting our Hail Marys.

Even though I had not attended All Souls Day service in decades, this invitation to attend on November 2, 2000, rekindled memories of my youthful religious zealotry.

Back then, sanctimonious as I was, I could really work the religion.

And, since I was bucking for MVAB (Most Valuable Altar Boy), as well as for a heavenly reward, I was prepared to avail myself of a special rule on All Souls Day.

Our priest, Father Fritz, told us that All Souls Day was the only day of the year that you could get a soul out of purgatory just by saying one short prayer—at least that was my understanding.

This short prayer on All Souls Day, and only on that day, would earn a *plenary indulgence*, or an immediate release/commutation of a soul's fiery, painful sentence in purgatory. One's allotted time in purgatory depended upon the number of venial sins committed but not confessed to the priest during Holy Confession (the Sacrament of Penance).

Or, in the case of more serious mortal sins, there had to be atonement after the confession was made. This would usually be good works, and additional prayers beyond the usual few that the priest would assign to be recited after one left the confessional booth.

If one died having confessed a mortal sin for which atonement had not been completed, then, the atonement must be *burned off* in purgatory. The duration of the suffering and purification depended on the mortal sin. For instance, there would be less time served for willfully eating a hot dog on Friday, with full knowledge of the eternal consequence sequestered in that tasty, salty, greasy morsel—than for say, murdering your father.

One could also offer up, for atonement, whatever suffering that life might bestow. This belief presented the possibility that the community of believers might ignore or even root for a sinner's suffering since suffering before death was preferred to fiery pain in the afterlife.

My brother, Paul, the family storyteller and comic, once came home from the confessional saying his atonement (penance) was to make a pilgrimage to Lourdes, France, on his hands and knees—though he could presumably take a ship from New York to cross the Atlantic above water. Noah would be proud.

Finally, as a LAST RESORT, one could say a perfect act of contrition without the sacrament of Penance—confessing to a priest, in order to remove the sentence of hell for a mortal sin.

However, perfection was defined as being contrite because one had offended God, and not because one feared the everlasting pain and suffering of hell. Possible, but in one's dying utterances of regret, it might be hard to push the hellfire thing from one's intentions.

I used to fear that at the end of my young life I might be in a car accident, splattered on the highway, watching my blood drain down the storm sewer grate and somehow have to conjure up a perfect act of contrition not because I feared the everlasting fires of hell ... oh no, no, no. Rather, my chief regret as I breathed my last breath, in my ninth year of life, would be that I had annoyed my all-powerful God.

So best to go to confession and play it safe.

On days other than November second, a specific, finite amount of time was removed from one's purging/purifying sentence as a result of prayers said by a departed soul's surviving loved ones and the collective members of the worldwide Church. For instance, maybe three or four hours of prayer and attending Mass might get a soul a year off time served.

But the formula was a complicated one. An intricate balancing scale was applied: the length of the prayer, the difficulty of getting to Mass, and perhaps, whether one placed a pebble in one's shoe while walking to church—suffering got you a big payoff in the Catholic Church.

Since there was this loophole that figuratively put the gates of purgatory on a swivel

I figured out that there was no reason why a devout person, like me, couldn't go into the church to pray several times on All Souls Day.

One prayer, I thought, on All Souls Day. Only one! All you had to do was just go into the church, say one prayer, and then:

Bingo!

A poor soul was sprung from the terrible suffering in purgatory.

So, on those November seconds of the past, I woke up, on the morning of All Soul's Day, a pasty-faced liberator of the flaming multitudes.

I 'd walk into church, bless myself with holy water, go down the aisle, genuflect, stand up, step into the pew, kneel down, and recite:

May the souls of the faithful departed, through the mercy of God, rest in peace. Amen.

Then I'd stand up, move from the pew into the aisle, genuflect, bless myself, stand up, turn around, walk back up the aisle, out the door of the church, wait a moment, then make an about face, and go back in again to start the process all over.

I would proceed in and out of church: back and forth, all day long.

I began by praying for the souls that I knew, and that I was pretty sure would get into heaven, but maybe had not been chosen on the first pick.

I knew how bad it felt not being chosen first for a playground ball game—and I was not on fire at the time.

Next, I would pray for the souls of the people that we thought were a cinch to get into heaven, just in case. First on my list were the old women from the Christian Mothers' Society, then the men who had been church ushers for years, and those older parishioners who would kneel, head bowed, devout, praying the rosary all during Mass.

And finally, I would focus on the largest group. The ones who I thought just might finish out the twentieth century in purgatory.

As the late, great Gamble Rogers used to say,

You live in a small town you know what everyone is doing, but

you read the paper anyhow to see who got caught at it.

Since this largest group took a lot of time, I determined it necessary to improve my efficiency in order to maximize the number of souls that I could deliver.

I couldn't move any faster down the church aisle without disrespecting the presence of the Holy Sacrament in the tabernacle so I had to shave seconds off of my time in other ways.

For instance, I realized at about the fiftieth or fifty-second liberated soul that after genuflecting, instead of standing up, and stepping into the pew, and kneeling down, that I could, from that low point of genuflection, without standing up, just do a bit of a side-squat slide over to the kneeler and then quick back over to the aisle again, and then down and up. I had perfected the reverse genuflection!

I think that if you spell genuflection backward it's, *noitcelfuneg*, which might just be Norwegian for:

Not much fun.

Back in my office, with those departed souls and Noah's Ark in the back of my mind I shook loose from my liturgical and biblical reveries. I walked outside and took some tomato stakes and bean poles down for the winter. After feeding the horses, the office beckoned, so I settled into some of the day's tedium.

My first task was to clear my answering machine.

I let the machine rewind and then set it to play. The first voice was that of my nephew, John, from California. John is the only child of my sister, Diane. Diane and I were the babies of the family, her being the baby girl and me the baby boy. I was eight years younger. Our mother worked at the typewriter factory for some years when we were young. Our two older sisters, Donna and Georgia, and our brother, Paul, were already married and not living at home. So, Diane and I grew up together.

She taught me how to tie my shoes. I helped her by placing my finger on the Christmas wrapping ribbon so she could knot and curl the bow, that sort of thing.

When I was six years old we had a business venture together: digging grub worms out of the manure in the cow yard. We sold the worms to local fishermen. Diane used the money to buy dress material so she could have nice clothes to wear to high school.

Diane didn't want to touch the worms. She would turn the odorous material over with a barn fork and shake all of the manure onto the ground. My job was to pick through the cow dung, grab the worms, and drop them into a bucket.

I loved the work and thought I had the easiest and most interesting part of the job.

I never knew what surprises I might find in the juicy manure, so there was great suspense. Forkful after forkful would yield nothing.... And then, one, two, three, or the jackpot—a half dozen or more little grubs. They looked like little sepulchers: white as pearls on the outside but filled with decayed excrement, and corruption.

My other job was to watch for cars driving down the gravel road which passed our farm. If the dust boiled up, it meant a car was coming. It might be her boyfriend who lived in town, so upon my alert signal, "CAR!" Diane would run into the barn so as not to be seen working in a barnyard, a ragged little kid squatting in the manure at her side.

Diane grew up before I did. She would share some of her adventures from the fascinating world of teen-land. When I was in eighth grade, she taught me how to dance. The most modern piece of furniture in our dining room was a big, blonde-wood hi-fi record player that we thought to be very hi-tech. Diane had done a lot of research. She had saved up to buy the machine that played 33 ⅓ albums as well as 45's with a diamond needle so that we could all experience the rich, full voices of Connie Francis and Frankie Avalon.

We had a linoleum floor in the dining room, smooth for dancing. Diane had a part-time job as a dance instructor at an Arthur Murray Dance Studio. She taught me the Cha-Cha, the Rumba, the Fox Trot, the Swing and, of course, the Twist.

When Saint Peter's School had that most improbable of events, the co-educational, eighth-grade dance, it was not only approved of, but organized by our teaching nuns. That the Sisters of the Immaculate Conception would encourage boys to hold the fullness of human girls in our arms was yet another mystery to add to the list of mysteries taught by our Holy Mother, The Church (as our Parish priest often called Her).

On that blessed evening, I danced every dance—all the dances Diane had taught me.

Diane had set out for California in her early twenties. She was the romantic one of our family, as my mom used to say:

**You and Diane, you're like the May side of the family.
The Mays just like to get in the car and go.**

In fact, my mother's observation describes my life as a traveling storyteller—a vocation impossible without enjoying the driving.

Diane moved to California after her son, John, was born. She did not find life easy in California. She was a single parent for most of that time, raising her son John by herself, usually in service jobs at hotels. Diane had been a waitress, a maître d', and a manager of various small concessions, usually in posh hotels—the Beverly Hills Hotel and the Beverly Wilshire.

When we visited her or she came home, she delighted in telling stories about celebrities she had met at work, like the time Frank Sinatra came in and gave her, the bartender, and the maître d' each a crisp one hundred dollar bill as a tip. She loved rubbing elbows with that glamorous life and then telling us back-home folks about it. Later, after the Beverly Hills Hotel was sold and older workers were laid off, she moved to Las Vegas where servers could always find work in the hotels and casinos.

The tape crackled a bit on the answering machine and then I heard my nephew John's voice again.

Uncle Jim, this is John from California. I think my mom might have liver and pancreatic cancer.

Just like that, in the blink of an eye, the day, the moment, everything changed.

Our lives on a thread, we live at the whim of tragic phone calls, messages from state police or doctors, or uniformed soldiers at the door with life-shattering bad news:

... This is the state police, there's been an accident.

... The lump is malignant.

... The United States Government regrets to inform you ...

John continued; "Uncle Jim, I'm in Las Vegas at Desert Springs Hospital. Please give me a call."

My wife, Nan, was standing in the office doing some work as the machine intoned: "End, new messages."

Oh my God Jim ... Call! Call! Find out what's happening!

But I could not. At that moment, I just could not do it. I was back in the Noah's Ark story, in my own deluge.

I was swimming against a flood of words for which I had not yet conceived images.

No, no. I think that I'm just going to go and do some errands. I'll be going out there as soon as I can. I think I need to do some errands first.

Since then, I've remembered my mother getting a Sunday morning call from the hospital that our father had died. She immediately began dusting the tables, lamps, and chairs throughout our house. When it's too hard to think then one has to do something to create some semblance of normalcy.

I did drive slowly, calmly, into town to pick up a few things I might need for my trip to Las Vegas.

Home again, I called Desert Springs Hospital. Diane answered her room phone. She sounded fine. She sounded like herself.

"Diane, what's going on?"

"Well, Jim, it looks like I'm on my way out."

And we cried.

I asked her if she knew anything about hospice. "No."

Well, we'll talk about that when I get there. I think I'll be there tomorrow. I'll get a plane as soon as I can.

Ok.

During the flight, I wondered if I could handle this time at my sister's bedside. The news seemed dismal. I had friends and colleagues who had experienced long, lingering deaths. I had been ashamed that I did not visit with them in time. I had meant to, but too often I would get news of their death, and deeply regret my failure to say good-bye. I almost always went to their funerals.

I have learned that the fear of not knowing what to do or say at the dying person's bedside is what kept me away. What kind of conversation does one have at the bedside of a dying family member or beloved friend? The two of you have, perhaps, walked similar paths and now one of you has been stricken, and the other spared. It's as though two people were strolling down a sidewalk on a sunny day and a piano fell out of a fourth-floor window, crushing only one.

How can someone stand next to a friend who is tied to a railroad track while the train is bearing down, all the while knowing the knots cannot be loosened?

And now, my sister Diane.... What would I be able to say to comfort her?

As my plane approached Las Vegas, I could see the distant city lights forming one tiny rhinestone in the black desert night below. Somewhere in that sparkling city, America's playground, my sister lay waiting for something that would crawl hungry out of the dark.

I'd stowed my luggage in the back, so I was the last one to deplane. I saw my nephew John ahead of me, looking around the corner at the end of the jetway just as I dropped my carry-on.

I turned to pick it up and heard a laugh as John had a direct, unobstructed view of my backside. John and I have this joke about, "Who got the Weber butt?"

The Weber butt is bigger than the May butt. John and I, and my sister Donna—we got the Weber butt. I was glad to begin this ordeal with a laugh and a hug from John.

He's an aspiring actor, tall and lanky, always the comic of the family. He had recently scored a major national commercial ad campaign on network television.

Back home all his cousins would stay up after the ten o'clock news to watch it.

Yep. He's got Uncle Shorty's eyes.

I'm proud of him. He's following his dreams, like his mom:

Diane, a small town girl that just picked up and left for California.

We walked through a maze of slots, roulette wheels, and the noise of payoff bells, buzzers, and whistles.

We were in a place like no other, a place that seemed out of step with our purpose—Las Vegas airport, a casino with runways and planes, the clanking, neon, adult party capital of the world. The patrons looked more worried and numb than happy and light-hearted, as they robotically pulled the levers on the slots. Making our way through the smoke, and over the soft patterned carpeting, it seemed that the ceiling was just a little bit too close to the floor.

Outside, the desert night wore a soft, rosy glow from the lights on The Strip as we walked through the airport parking lot—relief from the noise and neon.

I asked John how he was doing. He stopped, looked at me, choked up a bit, and threw his long, basketball-player arms in the air in different directions.

I can't believe this shit.

And then we walked some more. I wondered how I was going to get through the next few days.

Desert Springs Hospital was not located at a desert spring. It resided in a working class, bungalow neighborhood, a one-story hospital. As we entered, we were greeted by the smell of hospital air, some combination of disease, disinfectant, fear, and trouble.

We signed in and received visitor passes at the information desk. We walked down a long tile hallway, past the nurses' station, past families sitting in chairs, and into Diane's room.

She looked like herself, wearing a bright, red headband, ever the fashionable teenager, ready to bounce into her first new car—it was a 1955 tomato and cream Chevy with a Continental kit on the back. She was happy to see me. A big, welcoming smile set us at ease.

John's mother-in-law, Ani, and later his wife, Mayda, were at Diane's bedside. We had a good visit with her that night. She was lucid, answering the phone as friends and our sisters called. She told me:

I'm ready to see the angels.

She told me the songs she wanted sung at her funeral. I almost stopped her funeral planning. It seemed too soon. Then I caught myself, took out a notepad, and wrote down her requests:

**"Ave Maria," "Panis Angelicus," and
"On this day O beautiful Mother,"**

The three songs that she was often asked to sing for weddings at our hometown Catholic Church in Spring Grove. And, she said,

**I want Father Bill, that silver-haired, good-looking priest at
Saint Viator's to say my funeral Mass.**

We wanted to stay overnight in her room, but the nurse said that it was against hospital policy.

When we returned in the morning, we were told that Diane had been awake and anxious much of the night.

She'd gotten scared and hadn't rested.

And so we told the nurses that we were going to stay from then on, that we weren't going to leave her alone again.

The nurses said okay.

We met the doctor that first morning, a young man in his forties. He wore a polo shirt and sneakers. He seemed open and generous. When we became more familiar, he could tell us stories about his kids' soccer teams at a moment's notice. Diane liked him and he liked her.

He had come to the hospital on the Sunday night that she was admitted with a minor stroke brought on by the cancer's progress. He had come to see that she was settled in and he had even gone down to the gift shop in the hospital to buy her some dental floss, which she could never ever be without.

Maybe her doctor realized, even then, that this small favor would be the last thing that he would be able to do for her.

He had a clipboard full of papers: charts, reports, and results of tests. Holding that clipboard, he was like a statistician on a baseball team with those numbers: percentages, protocols, treatments, results of MRIs, blood scans, and white and red blood counts. He could tell us anything that we wanted to know. None of the information was good. None of it had anything to do with my sister getting well.

Hospitals are places for getting well, but she was not there for that purpose. She was not a good fit. But the hospital just kept rolling forward with its procedures. That's what hospitals do.

We took turns keeping company with Diane in the hospital. Mayda had to work, but John and Ani took the day shift and I was on the night shift. I slept in the chair beside her bed. Getting a good night's rest in a hospital is like trying to sleep in a small manufacturing plant. Beepers, bells, buzzers, floor buffers, and whistles all have their important duties to discharge during the overnight hours. Nurses and tech assistants moved in and out of Diane's room at all hours of the night. Their muted voices and the constant activity in the hallways, added to the random machine noises, meant our sleep was fitful at best. Though their work was necessary and we knew their intentions were good, interruptions were just frequent enough to prevent deep sleep.

About the time we'd get to sleep something would awaken us. The IV bag would empty, triggering a little beeper. A nurse's assistant would come in and turn off the beeper. Then, when we would finally get back to sleep the RN would come in to change the bag, and we'd be wide-awake. After she left, the whole process of trying to get some sleep would begin again.

Sometimes, the respiratory therapist came in and woke Diane up to "exercise those lungs," as he liked say. There wasn't anybody on the staff that expected my sister to live more than a few weeks, but somehow the hospital deemed it necessary to wake her up, to interrupt what moments of peace she had left, to *exercise those lungs*. The respiratory therapist would slap a clunky plastic mask over her nose and mouth, then open a valve in the plastic pipe works over her bed, allowing what appeared to be a cold, white mist to wind its way down the tube, and into the mask.

I heard the doctor tell the therapist to raise the bed to a certain upright angle, but I would always have to remind him to do so. Once Diane was awake, sitting upright and huffing along, the respiratory therapist would go out into the alley and smoke a cigarette.

Some nights were wonderful. We'd have long talks. We laughed about our childhood on the farm. I was a pest of a little brother, following her and her high school girlfriends around and interrupting their private conversations, probably concerning boys and cigarettes. Once they got so annoyed, they threw pebbles at me.

I could usually get my sister to buy me a guilt-inspired dinner when I brought up the pebble-throwing incident, and we laughed hard about it one night at the hospital.

Our German-American and Midwestern reserve fell away and we spoke of our love for each other in ways we had never done before. Sometimes she would just look at me and stroke my beard.

She spoke of spiritual matters—of attending morning Mass at St. Viator's Chapel, located on Flamingo Road, each day.

John, Ani, and I were glad we stayed with her in the hospital. We didn't do anything special. We were just there with her. Though we began this journey with Diane fearing that we would struggle to find the right words, we discovered that we only needed to be there, in her presence, and offer to pitch in when needed.

The end-of-life is a time when the intuitive, compassionate heart trumps language. She seemed to get better care the longer we stayed. Nurses would remark that she had a lovely, supportive family.

The staff at the hospital became more and more generous the longer we stayed. The first night they would not let me stay overnight. By the end of the week, they offered me the empty bed next to Diane's.

Our older sisters, Georgia and Donna, arrived in a matter of days.

We had a decision to make, one that Diane could not legally or ethically decide for herself. By that point in her illness, she was on strong pain medication and suffered strokes that interfered with her cognitive abilities. Among the cruelest things that Diane's cancer did was to increase the protein level in her blood, making it more sticky and prone to clots.

Her first mild stroke had brought her to the emergency room and her initial admittance to the hospital. Her second stroke, about a week later, made it hard for her to speak and robbed her of a portion of her awareness—taking her away from us sooner than the cancer alone might have.

Her son, John, would have the crushing and solemn duty of signing the legal documents to suspend all but palliative care (hospice), but John, of course, wanted the counsel of his aunts and uncle before signing anything.

Diane's primary doctor gave us no hope. The biopsy showed advanced, malignant lesions in her liver and pancreas.

The staff at the hospital seemed to accept, as a matter of course, that there existed no state-of-the-art cancer care in Las Vegas.

People came to Las Vegas to spend money and vacation; if they got sick, they went home to get the care they needed. In the year 2000, folks with cancer were more likely to come to Las Vegas for one last fling than for a cure. The working people who lived in Las Vegas had to go to Los Angeles for the best cancer treatment. We were agonizing over the decision of whether or not to move her to the UCLA Hospital. We decided to consult another doctor, considered to be the best oncologist in Las Vegas.

The doctor met with us late in the afternoon, about 4:00 pm. He entered the consultation room slowly, without speaking. He was a middle-aged oncologist who showed the exhaustion of fighting the heavyweight champ of diseases for over twenty years.

He let out a long sigh as he settled into the chair at the head of the conference table.

"How can I help you?" he asked.

Of course, we only had one question:

Is there anything that can be done for our sister?

He leaned forward,

"Well, yeah! Yeah! Maybe we could have done something if she had done what I asked her to do two-and-a-half months ago."

That was the first we knew that she had consulted with him in the summer before her hospitalization.

"If she had gone for the biopsy then, we might have had a protocol." He seemed miffed with what he seemed to consider her insubordination.

I countered, "Doctor, I know my sister chose to handle this in her own way, and she was probably in some sort of denial, but please be careful how you speak of her."

He looked at me for a long while, leaned back in his chair and became softer. "No, there really is no treatment protocol. There's literally nothing we can do here. We could take her to UCLA. I don't know how we would get her there. The long ambulance drive would be difficult, and the air ambulance is very expensive."

There's always the money—in our medical system we have to weigh the lives of our loved ones against financial ruin.

That our sister's survival—or at least a chance at it—might be denied due to money seemed barbaric to Donna, Georgia, and me. It seemed to scorn the dignity of our beloved sister—or any person.

We learned later

that her union, Service Employees International Union (SEIU), would have paid for an air ambulance to UCLA hospital and the best cancer care on the West Coast.

The doctor continued, "There is a possibility of a stroke if we airlift her, and once we get her to UCLA, there are really no protocols that fit her situation. The protocols that they do have there are very experimental. The numbers are not good, and some are painful."

The room quieted. We could hear the phone ringing at the desk outside the door. Someone laughed and said, "How good of you to call."

I asked, "Doctor, what would you do?"

This question seemed to energize him. He leaned forward in his chair.

What would I do?
What would I do?
First of all, my family will not have to make this decision.
I've already written everything up.
What would I do?
Knowing the situation she's in?
Knowing the disease, and knowing the state of medicine.
What would I do?
Put me on a beach and don't touch me.
That's what I'd do.

So, we found our sister a beach.

We admitted Diane to the Nathan Adelson Residential Hospice, in Las Vegas. The mission statement of Nathan Adelson Residential Hospice read:

No one should end the journey of life alone, afraid, or in pain regardless of their ability to pay.

The facility was housed in a pagoda-style building with French doors that opened onto patios. It featured a central courtyard with a fountain, rose bushes dedicated to the memory of former residents, and an aviary so that grandchildren could play with the parakeets when they came to say goodbye.

If the beauty and style were not enough of a contrast to its somber, yet sacred work, it was located down the street from the Luxor Casino and around the corner from the Hard Rock Café.

The building was divided into pods, each containing four patient rooms. There was a family room and kitchen to serve each pod. Visiting families and friends could cook, sleep on large couches, and have a comfortable place to gather so that they could remain at their loved one's side. Each individual room had sliding French doors to the outside.

The staff was very proud of those French doors and patios. During our preliminary tour, a staff member told us that they had brought a pony onto the patio of a little boy's pod.

Hearing this, my nephew, John, looked at me and said,

So this means life is serious, Uncle Jim?

John had been repeating this phrase, as his mother's health failed, and most poignantly, as he signed the forms to withhold all medical procedures other than palliative care.

I was watching John's initiation. He was leaving behind the son taken care of by his mother and occupying the man taking care of his mom.

Years later, at the National Storytelling Festival in Jonesborough, TN, an old Jesuit priest approached me after hearing me tell this story about Diane.

Do you know the origin of the word palliative?

No Father, but I'd like to know.

"Palliative care," the old cleric whispered—his demeanor gentle, deferential, not unlike my memories of kind priests in the confessional—"comes from the Latin for the covering or cloak, because the shepherd would take his pall, his cloak, and cover the sick lamb—to keep it warm and safe."

Nathan Adelson Hospice became our shepherd, as it wrapped

our sister in its tender care. My sisters Donna and Georgia stayed at the hospice to get Diane's room ready with flowers and CDs for the CD player—Paul Anka, and the Three Tenors.

I drove back to the hospital to meet the medical transfer crew. While we were waiting, I said to Diane,

We're moving out of here. We're going to a party.

She smiled and said,

Good.

Soon the medical transfer team burst into the room, all business, looking young and fit: the men were ripped, the women had big, feathered hair. They rolled in a gurney, jacked it up, slid my sister onto it, and covered her up. Then they sped out the door, and down the hall at a trot.

Soon we were out in the sunshine, Diane gliding across the parking lot. Up went the gurney again. It slid into the back of a specially equipped van. I jumped into the van with Diane. Someone closed the door.

As the van sped through Las Vegas traffic, Diane lay on the gurney holding the end of her blanket under her chin. Her eyes alive, she smiled at me and said,

I love this!

She always did like to travel.

She was transferred to a wheelchair at the hospice. We wheeled her around the place; showed her the aviary and the central courtyard with the fountain and memorial rose garden.

Donna and Georgia welcomed us to her flower-strewn room, with Paul Anka, singing "Diana" on the CD player. Diane loved Paul Anka and would always go see his shows in Las Vegas.

It seemed that we had come to an oasis, a rest stop. There wasn't hospital trouble in the air, but rather a gracious and compassionate acceptance of the natural order of things.

The hospice recalled those rainy-gray summer days of youth when everything slowed down. I stayed in my house on such days. No baseball, fishing, or romping through the woods. I invited my boyhood friends over and we played long, slow board games and talked to my mother while she ironed—the smell of damp laundry mingled with the rain-fresh air coming through the open screen windows.

Diane's hospice team managed her pain with great care and expertise. They assured us that patients do not have to suffer from the physical pain that cancer brings, as patients did in years past. But there is a price to pay, a trade off. Toward the end of her life, Diane could not speak. We watched her carefully for any physical signs that she might be in pain: cringing, grimacing, or shifting position in her bed frequently. If she'd behave in one of these ways, we'd call for the nurse. The nurse would arrive promptly, administer more morphine, and then Diane would relax again. On these occasions, we would thank the nurse, grateful both for the quick response and for the drug. However, under the influence of the morphine, whatever awareness—a smile, a squeeze of the hand—that Diane showed before, seemed to diminish. She'd leave us and we'd feel lonesome.

Sometimes, under the influence of the morphine, Diane would

reach for someone next to her at the wall on the other side of the bed, where no one stood. She moved slowly on these occasions, like swimming through honey.

Nearly every day I read from a book called: *The Tibetan Book of Living and Dying* by Sogyal Rinpoche.

The book contains a compilation of Tibetan Buddhist teachings for individuals and their loved ones as they proceed through the final stages of living. Born and raised in Tibet, Sogyal Rinpoche studied under some of the greatest and most knowledgeable lamas, but he also studied and worked in the West.

Based upon the *Tibetan Book of the Dead*, his book has become a kind of *Tibetan Book of the Dead (Lite)* for westerners. A friend had given it to me some years ago after we experienced a death in the family. I had never read it, but I had gotten the courage to throw it in my suitcase while packing for Las Vegas. It became a handbook for me, a guide, both practical and profound, as our sister declined.

The Tibetan Buddhists honor death as a very important part of life—a sacred passage that must be nurtured and blessed.

Taking my cue from the Tibetan text during those last few days, I would bring my lips right to Diane's ear and say:

You know, you're heading toward that light, toward God.

Really?

Oh yeah! You're heading toward God, and love, and that light, and Mom will be there and Dad. They'll all be there.

Really?

**Certainly! You've loved so many people in your life and now all
that love and more will come back to you.**

Over the days that I had been with her, streams of people came
through to visit. Many were work friends she had met as a server
at the casino: other waitresses, dishwashers, bouncers, and
bartenders. Most would say that,

**We don't know what we're going to do without Diane.
We would always go to her when we needed to
talk something through. ...**

One friend of Diane's, a hairdresser, who was raising her child
by herself, told a story:

**Yeah, when I was pregnant, Diane made me drink lemon
water until I was goofy. And then she kept playing Mozart
because she was afraid my country music would make the baby
depressed.**

Once, when this same hairdresser friend was visiting, she
and I were talking quietly as Diane seemed in a deep sleep. I
mentioned that perhaps a community college program could
help her qualify for a better job than the beauty business. At this
Diane open her eyes wide, nodded and carefully pronounced an
emphatic

Yes!

I had to return home to Illinois for a short time to take care of
some business. On the airplane home I remembered my fears
on the flight to Las Vegas some weeks earlier—that I would
not know what to do or what to say to my sister as she awaited
death—tied to a railroad track, so to speak. But, I've come to

realize that

we all live between the rails, with death, the locomotive, always coming our way.

Some, perhaps, just have a better idea of the train's schedule.

On the flight home I knew I belonged back at Nathan Adelson Hospice with my sister, not home, not anywhere else.

As Diane failed and continued to lose fluids, her face took on the shape of many of our old aunts, and cousins. Her final passage seemed to somehow connect her with all the generations of our family. It seemed one more reminder that we all are connected. That death is something we all have in common. We all have to do this final act if we are to complete this human journey.

After three weeks or so with Diane, as Thanksgiving approached, I had to return home for a couple days to finish some business and check in with my wife, Nan, and our family. At home, catching up with my work, I'd also made plans for Nan and me to return to Las Vegas as soon as we could. We'd prayed and hoped that our family could be together for one more Thanksgiving.

While I was away, my nephew, John, called each day to brief me about his mom's condition.

Yeah, you know, she's slipping each day.

Of course, this was expected, monitored even, by the descending level of fluid in her catheter bag.

It was a sort of cruel joke on the Noah story. The story that I continued to think about: in the story of the great flood the receding waters had brought great hope—but in Diane's case they brought only a grim confirmation.

However, in the absence of hope our family was buoyed by the deep, unifying power of resignation and grief. Diane's impending death was like a dark and terrible storm that we faced together. It brought increased measures of attention and kindness, as if the storm would sweep us away if we did not hold onto one another.

So, our family welcomed the dehydration and its gifts. John had signed for the removal of the IV bag.

On one call, I heard anguish in John's voice,

Yeah, she won't keep her hospital gown on anymore. She keeps taking it off—so here she is, like a diapered baby.

"It's fine John. I think you did the right thing. We'll be there as soon as we can, for sure by Thanksgiving. What do the doctors say about Diane holding out for Thanksgiving with the family?"

The doctors didn't want to say much of anything. But she made it.

Our family cooked a turkey in the hospice's family kitchen just outside Diane's room. The turkey had a comforting aroma, reminiscent of the happy Thanksgivings of our childhood.

The day after Thanksgiving, I sat out in the courtyard with my rosary beads. I had learned to pray again. Praying was a way to feel close to all of the life forces, divine and otherwise, without having to think. It allowed a certain communing with death's dark, mysterious domain—while soothing the fear and the pain.

In the *Tibetan Book of Living and Dying*, it is said that prayer is not only speaking to the Divine. Rather, prayer is the Divine.

The book also spoke repeatedly about the importance of staying in the moment. At one point I read that:

This is all we have, this moment of life and goodness—this moment. Don't be thinking about the future, or worrying about the future, but if you must, if you must place your attention on the future, if you must think, and worry, and be concerned about that, if you must, then think about the absolute certainty and unpredictability of the moment of your death. And that will get you back into the present.

Our time together at the hospice with Diane and our family was one long string of dear moments that we knew we would never have again. These moments were like pearls strung together by necessity and burnished by love and loss.

On Diane's last day, I sat in the rose-scented courtyard, spelling myself in the fresh air. I heard a cackle. I looked up and spotted a raven which had landed in the Eucalyptus tree above me.

I hadn't seen a raven the whole time that I'd been out in Las Vegas. I fancy myself a pretty good birder and would have noticed. I pondered the rascal perched on a branch, clucking and mumbling, picking at seeds. Looking at me, the raven turned his head to this side and that. He emitted a brief caw now and then.

I thought of the mysterious flight of the raven in the Noah story. Perhaps all ravens seemed mysterious, I mused. We continued watching each other: He watched. I wondered.

A few minutes later my cell phone rang. My nephew's voice: Uncle Jim, I think you'd better get in here.

I hurried back to Diane's room. The pace of her breathing had changed. I'd been counting the spaces between her breaths for days.

We watched as her breath became more and more shallow. John stood on one side of the bed, holding her hand. I stood on the other side of the bed with my hand on her forehead. We witnessed her breath move up into her throat, quicken, and then become wisps of air, like soft wings brushing across her dry lips.

Finally, her lips gently nipped at the last, tiny breath, as if clutching a bit of dear life for a moment more. Then she became profoundly still—a stillness beyond understanding.

During all this time, death certainly had a presence in her room, but death did not seem to be stalking her—more a wolf curled up, asleep in a corner.

When the wolf did gently pounce, it came to her less as a beast than a merciful angel.

**"Ave Maria" played on the CD player as she left us—
paean for a queen.**

We had that funeral at St. Viator's as she requested, with "Ave Maria," "Panis Angelicus" (Bread of the Angels), and "On this day O beautiful Mother" sung by the parish soloist; and that good-looking, silver-haired priest, Father Bill, said Mass.

My nephew, John, eulogized his mom. He said that she was the best person he had ever known, and that he wished he had told her so more often.

I placed her urn and ashes in a brand new Wilson gym bag,

carried her on board the airplane, placed the bag in the overhead and told her,

Diane, we're going home to Spring Grove.

We had another funeral at St. Peter's in December. *Ave Maria* was sung by Diane's cousin, Nick, up in the choir loft where she had stood on young legs, singing that very song for weddings.

After the funeral Mass we formed a quiet procession to the cemetery, past the Grotto of Our Lady of Fatima, and across the Nippersink Creek as the church bell tolled a mournful cadence that echoed cold stone over the village. I had asked Father to let the church bell toll in the tower until we were beside Diane's grave. We buried Diane at the foot of our mother's and father's graves, just downhill from both sets of grandparents. The bell continued to toll, clear and sorrowful in the razor-sharp air, even as Father read the prayers at her graveside.

The parish priest of our childhood, Father Plesa, had been reassigned to St. Peter's just in time to say Diane's funeral Mass. He had known our family in the 50s when he was a young assistant priest. Diane practically swooned in his presence then and thought it a waste that he couldn't marry. He served his people and parishes faithfully, a devout, eloquent, and kind man.

In spite of the cold, Father did not wear an overcoat while he read the prayers—instead his long black cassock and white surplice mirrored the frozen black soil and patches of white snow on the surrounding farm fields. Our LA sister was home.

Father stood there, an elegant and consoling emissary of this sometimes comforting, enduring, old religion that promises something more than this ending—this lowering into cold, frozen ground. Behind our priest, rows of headstones reminded us that we were not alone in our grief.

The Mystery of Noah's Raven

My sister's death, and the appearance of the raven on her last day has cast, for me, a new role for Raven in the Noah's Ark story.

Raven seems a mystery in that story of the Great Flood.

In one version of Genesis, it reads that Raven was sent out by Noah. Nothing further is stated.

In another version, scripture reads only that Raven flies to and fro.

In contrast, Noah releases the dove on the first day of the storm's end. The dove returns—there is no place to land; everything is submerged.

Sent out on the second day, the dove returned with an olive sprig in its beak, which filled all with hope. The gentle bird had found land upon which to rest.

On the third day, the dove does not return. The bird had found dry land and a permanent home. The Ark and humanity were spared.

So the dove's journey is clearly played out, but there's nothing about Raven. Where does Raven go?

I would like to think that Raven made a choice.

That Raven chose to minister to the dying. That Raven decided not to stay with the relative security of the Ark (not even Noah's family could live forever) but to attend to those who were crossing over. He made a decision, just as we must: whether to stay in our carefully constructed Arks, keeping the idea of death at bay, or whether to stand with our loved ones when they are at that lonely, frightening, blissful brink—that natural, and inevitable threshold that we all must cross and for which we all need guidance.

Raven, in his requiem cloak, here seems the comforter. Sitting on the wrist of La Muerte[2] like some death hawk of God, he rises from his safe perch and flies on ebony wings, beneath gray clouds of grief to dispense balm to the dying, and then back again, with the hoarse, raspy assurances of our loved ones waiting for us on the other side.

And if his example foreshadows an opportunity to spend time with those that we love as they face death, and that someone graces our bedside—stands vigil when our time comes.... If Raven's teaching means that we have that window of opportunity to experience a unique and deep love that may not be possible at any other time in our life, and to find a certain courage—then I say we embrace that opportunity.

I say we take our chances with the Raven.

Chapter 8

Failures, Wounds, and Second Chances

King Arthur and Percival's Story[1]

In the Arthurian cycle of stories, Percival seeks the Holy Grail. At first, he seems an unlikely candidate because he is isolated in the forest, alone with his mother. She wishes to protect him, to keep him innocent, and to, above all, keep him away from Arthur and the Knights of the Round Table. Though Percival is of noble birth, his mother does not name him. Rather, she gives him names of endearment like *my dear one*. She fears for her son, because, unknown to Percival, his father and brother had died in King Arthur's service.

Alone in the natural world, with no companionship save his mother, Percival lives the life of the forest: hunting, fishing, and gathering. He roams free and swims in the rivers and lakes. He becomes a deadly hunter with lance and bow. But just as each person must leave his or her childhood, village, and mother, Percival must face his own destiny.

One day he is in the forest and hears thundering hooves. Making his way toward the sound, he comes to a road and sees two of Arthur's knights riding powerful chargers, their colorful banners snapping; their armor radiant.

He thinks they are gods. They laugh as he prostrates himself before them.

We are not gods, but Knights of King Arthur's Round Table.

However, to Percival, they seem divine. He decides to go to Arthur's court and join up. When he reveals his wishes to his mother, she is broken-hearted. Unable to dissuade him, she weaves for him a crude peasant cloak, and gives him an old pitiful plow horse to ride to Arthur's court, hoping these accoutrements will hide his nobility, and cause Arthur to reject his request to serve.

As he arrives at King Arthur's court, Percival meets a magnificent knight riding a sorrel (red) horse. The knight is carrying a red banner and wearing magnificent armor, also trimmed in crimson.

Percival asks the knight where he might obtain such a fine set of armor. The Red Knight laughs and tells him to go ask Arthur, and while he is there, to remind Arthur that none other than he, the Red Knight, has stolen a goblet from the round table, and spilled wine on Guinevere, the queen, to further the insult.

Percival proceeds to Arthur's castle to deliver this provocative message, this challenge to Arthur's reputation and authority.

Upon meeting Percival, Arthur immediately recognizes that the young lad is of noble birth, despite the fact that Percival is dressed in humble attire and that his mount is a broken-down workhorse. Percival recounts the Red Knight's message and asks how to join the Knights of the Round Table.

Sir Kay, Arthur's stepbrother, and a great warrior—though sometimes cruel and scheming—suggests that Percival go take the goblet from the Red Knight as a test of his worthiness to serve Arthur.

Arthur admonishes Sir Kay for this, knowing the boy has no training in combat. However, before anyone could stop him, Percival accepts the challenge and dashes off to confront the ominous Red Knight. Arthur sends a squire to try to intervene, but the squire is too late.

The Red Knight laughs at Percival's demands for the goblet and strikes him a playful blow up the side of his head with the flat of his sword, knocking Percival to the ground.

Angry, Percival grabs his hunter's javelin—a weapon that no self-respecting, chivalrous, knight would use—and throws it. The lance sails through the opening of the Red Knight's visor, through his eye socket, and out the back of his skull. He is dead before he hits the ground.

Percival thinks to himself,

This being a knight is not as hard as I thought it might be.

He returns the goblet to the stunned squire who has been watching from the distance. Percival dons the Red Knight's suit of armor, mounts the red horse, and lets the reins of the horse loosen so the horse and nature can take him where they will.

One day he wanders upon Lord Gornemant of Gohort, an old lord with a small kingdom who takes Percival on as an apprentice and becomes his first mentor. The Lord is appalled when he hears that the Red Knight has been unceremoniously killed from a distance with a hunter's spear, an undignified demise that shocks Arthur's court, as well. The Lord teaches Percival to fight with honor, allowing an opponent fair position. He also admonishes him to never kill unless necessary. He tells Percival that a proper knight places his sword at the throat of a vanquished enemy, and then offers to spare his life if that knight will present himself in service to Arthur and the Round Table.

The old Lord also tells Percival that it would be prudent to:

Stop asking so many questions. Listen to your elders and quit talking so much about your mother.

Percival learns very quickly. He has many adventures rescuing damsels, performing acts of chivalry, and gallantry wherever he travels.

But finally, worn down from long days of travel and combat, Percival finds himself hungry, tired, and in great need of rest. One day he wanders into a land that appears ravaged. The crops are withered in the field, the animals and women barren. Riding slowly through this parched land with little hope of finding rest and sustenance, he comes upon a nobleman and his servant.

The two sit in a boat on a lake. The nobleman is obviously in horrible pain, unable to do anything but lean against the side of his boat and fish. He tells Percival of his castle nearby and invites him to stay the night.

To Percival's surprise, he is greeted with deference at the castle. He is bathed, given clean clothes, and seated in an honored position at the banquet table. Before long, the great doors of the banquet hall burst open and a procession enters, led by a knight carrying a bloody lance. Behind the knight, carried in on a bejeweled dais, is the ailing nobleman, who Percival saw in the boat.

Percival soon learns that this man, who invited him to the castle, is the Fisher King, suffering from a wound from which he cannot heal—and yet, cannot die. In these stories, when the king is sick the kingdom is sick. The Fisher Kingdom is parched, nothing grows. The farm animals are barren and give no milk. No children are birthed. Percival now understands the devastation that he saw all around him before entering the castle.

The procession continues until a golden chalice is held aloft at the end of the cortège.

All bow before the Holy Grail. Food, drink, and all things sustaining flow from this chalice, a bottomless, shimmering vessel. Percival watches the scene with great interest—but remembering Lord Gornemant's admonition to not ask too many questions—Percival is silent, deciding to wait 'til morning for an explanation.

In the morning, he awakens to an empty castle. His horse and clothes are prepared, but everyone is gone.

〜〜〜

Percival travels back to the Round Table where Arthur receives him with the honor befitting the return of a conquering knight who has spared the lives of so many vanquished in battle— sending them to serve Arthur's Court.

Arthur proclaims a feast in honor of Percival. In the midst of this feast, an old hag rides into the middle of the merrymaking.

There's an abrupt silence as she reins in her skinny mule before the king. Most are repulsed and demand that this ugly old woman be sent away. But Arthur, who knows her to be the crone, Cundry, from whom he has periodically sought advice, asks her purpose.

**"Why are you having a feast at a time like this?" she cackles,
"when there is such suffering in the realm of The Fisher King."
"And worse, you honor him!"
She pointed a bony, dirty finger at Percival.**

Arthur counters that Percival is the finest young knight of the realm and cites his achievements.

"Do you know where he has been?" Queries Cundry.

Arthur sat silent.

"Do you know *who* he has seen? *What* he has seen?"

Arthur did not.

"Well?" She squawked, her voice echoing now in the silence of the stunned assemblage.

**"Percival has met the Fisher King,
the king whose wound cannot heal," Cundry hissed,
"who can neither live nor die!
Percival ate from the Holy Grail!
But did he ASK THE QUESTION?"**

Asking the question was his only task. Had he asked it, the Fisher King would have been healed. The rivers would flow again. Crops would grow. Women would bear children and the kingdom would be green and prosperous.

NO! He said NOTHING!

"And so now the suffering in the Fisher Kingdom is greater than it has ever been," said Cundry. With that, she turned the unsteady mule around and exited the great hall, all the while scowling and shaking her head from side to side.

Those gathered are horrified and scandalized. Inconsolable, Percival swears a solemn oath to return to the suffering realm of the Fisher King.

Percival promises that he will not sleep in the same bed on consecutive nights until he completes this quest; that he will be determined as a dogged wolf on a trail until he once again steps foot upon the parched wasteland of the suffering monarch. Percival is true to his word, though his journey is long and his suffering profound.

Finally, he reaches another defining moment of his life in the form of the Black Knight. The Black Knight is a force of nature. He rides a great black charger, and he attacks Percival, mounted on his red horse of power.

The battle is fierce. The two lock in deadly combat, each man coming to within a whisker of the reaper's sword until finally the two of them and their horses pitch over the edge of a ravine. The Black Knight is defeated. Percival's beloved horse breaks its neck and perishes. The powerful red horse that Percival has ridden since his passionate, youthful days of knighthood is gone.

Now he must ride the black horse that he earned with the terrible victory over the Black Knight and the sacrifice of his faithful mount. The black horse takes Percival to the Fisher King. Again, he encounters the king in the boat, who again invites Percival to a banquet.

Once again, Percival takes his place in the banquet hall as the procession enters: the knight with the bloody lance, the king carried on the dais, and the Chalice which Percival now knows, is indeed the Holy Grail.

But Percival is not the same knight. He has suffered failure, humiliation, and he is sick of battle and death. He has ridden the black horse—the requiem steed. The red horse of his youth, his passion, and perhaps, his false virility, is gone.

This time, Percival finds the suffering of the Fisher King heart-rending. Without even thinking, he approaches His Majesty, bows, and whispers:

Sire, what ails thee?

The Holy Grail becomes even more luminous, the Fisher King rises from his pallet on the dais with rejuvenated strength. He strides to the window where he looks out to see the land greening, trees blossoming. In the fields the cows begin to lactate, animals and children are conceived, and the land is healed. The banquet hall erupts in joyous celebration and Percival is hailed as a savior and the wisest and most gallant of them all.

∽

It seems that all that was necessary to heal the king and the kingdom was the asking of the GRAIL QUESTION:

Sire, what ails thee?

Brother Paul, Who Art Thou?

I am very lucky to have been guided by storyteller and friend, Elizabeth Warren, through the territory of the Grail legend of Percival. Thank you so much, Liz.

I first heard the story of King Arthur's Knight, Percival, not long after my older brother's death. My brother was, in many ways, royalty in our family.

Paul was a self-made man who started his own construction business. Clever, charming, and funny, he was known by everyone as the best storyteller in town. He'd do voices, speak in unknown languages, play pranks, invent nicknames for friends and workmates, and tell tall tales.

When I was in high school, and he had a young family, he got me a summer job as a union laborer with the company where he worked. The job paid my way through college.

While on the job, older workers would ask me if I was Paul May's brother. I soon learned that he was a celebrity at work, too. Sometimes they would ask about one of his famed stories—looking for mock corroboration, or just to have a little teasing fun.

One hot summer day I heard a big earth scraper rumbling along the curb behind me while I shoveled gravel. The big diesel engine gurgled and clanked to a stop. Silence rushed into the vacuum vacated by the diesel's roar. The operator sat high above me on the cushioned black leather seat of his massive steel machine. He was quiet at first, studying his entrance, preparing his comments.

He looked down at me over his mirrored sunglasses that were almost as blinding as his aluminum hard hat. "You Paul May's brother?"

"Yes."

"He's got more shit than a young robin. You know that?"

I laughed, knowing where this conversation was headed.

"Is he still raising those giant chickens?"

"Yep." I was game. I liked Paul's outlandish stories myself. Besides, we all worked hard, sometimes sweating ten to twelve hours a day in the summer sun with few breaks, and I was ready for some rest and distraction.

We laborers, and especially we younger ones, looked up to these machine operators, but the worksite was tense. Our work never seemed to rise to the level of the operators' and foreman's expectations. So, any pause, especially a humorous one, was a welcome respite from the usual sweat, work and worry of the day.

You know those giant chickens that your brother talks about?

I replied:

**Is the Pope Catholic? Does a bear shit in the woods?
I helped raise those chickens.**

I thought I could see a bit of a smile on my questioner's bristly face. The operator continued:

"Paul said he had an order for roosters from Suburban Oil (a local asphalt company). Yeah, he said that Suburban was going to cut the spurs off the legs of those giant roosters and use them for scarifier teeth on the graders to rip up the old blacktop roadways."

By now we were both laughing—our relative places on the company pecking order having evaporated.

At that point, I liked to continue Paul's story, respond to the challenge. I felt it incumbent on me to back up my brother, to uphold the family tradition of blue chip bullshitting.

Yeah, we had a pretty good year. Had that big rooster sale to Suburban and then we had to lease a six-wheeler gravel dump truck to haul a half dozen fryers over for the St. Peter's Church annual chicken dinner—they served three hundred dinners off those six young fryers.

~

Jeeze Louise, you're about as full of it as your big brother.

With that, he started up the big engine and roared off down the haul road, black smoke pouring from his stack as the machine picked up speed.

I could go back to work with the satisfaction that I had talked myself into being *one of the boys* on the crew.

~

To be assigned to operate a motor grader on an excavation crew was to be recognized as one of the most knowledgeable, most skilled men on the job. If you were like my brother Paul, considered the best young blade man in the company, you were practically a folk hero.

One summer morning, our crew was finishing the rough

(preliminary) grading of a roadbed. The young grader operator, the rookie blade man, had graded the gravel quantities and elevations as close to the blueprint specs as he could. We were having coffee, chatting, and waiting for another motor grader and a more experienced blade man to *finish*—complete the final grading with close tolerances.

Just then we heard the distant hum of a diesel engine. Looking up, we saw my brother Paul rumbling toward us in his motor grader, cruising along in high gear. Coming from another job, he was now arriving to put the final touches on the subgrade before we laid down the gravel. The dense black plume of the motor grader's diesel exhaust hung in the air over his motor grader like the mane of a thundering yellow charger, a noble steed who would respond to every nuance of his master's command.

Paul was our champion, our version of a medieval knight, much anticipated and welcomed at our gravel, blacktop, and concrete jousting tournament of road building. He made us laugh!

I reckon I was proud.

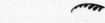

Paul had dropped out of high school at sixteen years of age. His first job in the construction trades was pushing a wheelbarrow of mortar up plank ramps on a building site to supply the bricklayers. The older laborers, who were pushing wheelbarrows in front of him, admonished him to slow down as he was running into their heels with his wheelbarrow.

He was always the hardest worker, always noticed by the foreman. Finally, Paul worked his way up to union grader operator. Later, the logical step, he started his own company.

When he was younger and still working for a boss, he got me a job with the company, Lakeland Construction. I'd sometimes ride to work with him if we were at the same job site. Early morning, he'd be waiting for me in the driveway, in his Ford pickup, motor running. I'd jump into the cab—a two-wheel drive little half-ton that, with Paul at the wheel, could go anywhere that the four-wheel drive models could.

The early morning drives were usually long. I welcomed the time to ease into the day. I'd settle into the seat, lean back and ready myself to hear a joke, a story about some guy who had really looked bad on one of the job sites, or maybe one of Paul's plans for the future—the smell of diesel fuel, grease, coffee, and Viceroy cigarettes—like incense to the god of construction and hard work.

I got four, sixty-dollar payments left on this pickup. After it's paid off I think I can buy the old grader that Bolander has up for sale—you know, get some side jobs with it. I already got PAUL MAY AND SONS painted on the side of the pickup."

His sons were still in diapers. I marveled at his ambition, though it should not have surprised me. We told a family legend about how Paul built himself a dirt track in the backyard when he was in elementary school. He'd run around in circles for hours, trying to stay thin so he could be a jockey someday.

In his proposal to his life-long bride, Judy, he said:

Stick with me and you'll be wearing diamonds.

Paul and Judy had five children. He helped his sons get operators union cards to work in the family business—Paul May and Sons Grading and Excavating—and helped his daughter start her own business.

He always pushed himself, partied as hard as he worked, rarely rested, and wore out his body by the age of 63.

I never asked my brother the Grail question:

What ails thee?

I never asked it even though I knew whatever drove him so hard was giving him no rest.

How often do we men ask this question of one another? How often do we ask it of our brothers, fathers, sons, friends, and colleagues?

So we seldom hear the painful stories.

In my brother's case, the story may have begun with a rigid Catholic school that could not see his genius. Never one to sit quietly at his desk while the teaching nun tried to manage and teach sixty to seventy children in one classroom, Paul suffered the beatings at school that were common in those days, especially for disobedient or restless boys.

My sister, Diane, told me she used to come home from school crying because, once again that day, all the kids had gathered around Father Fritz on the playground to watch while he paddled Paul.

Paul also felt the shame of being the son of a tenant farmer, moving to a new farm about every three years. He always wanted his own place.

Remembering my brother as I write here, my memory brimming, I wonder: what is it that gets in the way of any of us asking the Grail Question?

Perhaps fear at the prospect of hearing too much pain? Perhaps afraid someone else's pain will remind us of our own?

We men are programmed for success and dominance, so we are especially uncomfortable with taking on what might appear to be a tortured soul whom we cannot help. *So failure looms....*

BUT, the lesson of this King Arthur Grail story is that the hero, Percival, only has to muster enough compassion to ask the Grail Question:

Sire, what ails thee?

These simple words—this direct and innocent question, instinctively uttered by Percival, is all that is needed to heal the Fisher King.

Percival seems to have endured initiation by failure. His mentor, the old squire, Gorenmant, admonished him for his cowardly, though guileless, killing of the Red Knight. Cundry humiliates him in the presence of King Arthur for his failure to speak during his first visit to the Fisher King's domain. He lost his red horse of youth, and passion, and had to ride the black horse of death to the gate of the wasted kingdom. And yet, Percival somehow triumphs.

My brother, Paul, wanted me to be a lawyer. He never understood why I dropped out of law school at the University of San Diego, even though my grades were good. I told him I couldn't stand the weather in San Diego—nothing happening all the time.

He never quite got used to the idea of me being a storyteller. I don't think he ever realized (and I've just started to suspect it myself)—that I was, and am, just trying to be like him.

But, I know as sure as the Pope is Catholic, that if Paul May were alive today, I'd still be the second best storyteller from Spring Grove, Illinois.

And so, if this book, this *Trail Guide for a Crooked Heart,* had just one useful thing to say, it would be that we all take the time to ask our loved ones the question:

What ails thee?

The question itself, with its concern and compassion, with its interested attention to another human being, may be all that is required for healing to take place, or at least to begin a journey that sets out, at the trailhead, to ask:

Will you tell me your story?

It goes faster if you start.
—Anonymous worker

Acknowledgements

First and foremost, I thank my family for their ongoing love and support. Nothing is possible without all of you.

My deepest gratitude goes to Jay O'Callahan, who has believed in my particular point of view and in what artistry I may have. Heart-felt thanks go to you, Jay, for your friendship, your powerful leadership in our storytelling community, and for showing us what it means to be a consummate artist.

Thanks to Ted Parkhurst for recognizing that I had something to say in print, and Linda Parkhurst, for her kindness and artistic sensibilities.

A thank you to my beloved Blue Mountain Lake retreat group for years of deep friendship and support. It has been an honor to work and play with you.

I am forever indebted to all the storytellers—the ones I have met and those who, down through the centuries, have kept so many of these stories alive. Thank you for generously passing on your art and wisdom to me. This book is not possible without you.

If it hadn't been for my bright-faced and curious fourth and fifth-grade students at Clay Street Elementary in Woodstock, Illinois back in October of 1979, I might not have become a storyteller. Thanks for your attention and joy while listening to my first story. My gratitude also goes out to the thousands of students who have listened since that first story.

For all of you who attended The Illinois Storytelling Festival in Spring Grove for some twenty-three years: what a thrill to have you all come to my backyard to hear my stories and those of my storytelling colleagues.

Thanks to all those who have attended my workshops in Oaxaca, Mexico, in Harvard, Illinois, and around the country. Your ideas, courage and artistry have become much of the grist for this book. Thanks especially to Gail Permenter and Jennie Bartoline, who have helped me guide my summer solstice storytelling workshop in Harvard for some twenty years.

I want to thank everyone who read the manuscript, especially Nyla

Fujii-Babb, Jan Bosman, Carol Birch, Doug Elliot, Bill Harley, Beth Horner, Gwenda Ledbetter, Jay O'Callahan, Susan O'Halloran, Jim Pfitzer, Ed Stivender, Dovie Thomason, Liz Warren, and Megan Wells. Your encouragement and insights have been invaluable.

I want to particularly thank Jennie Bartoline for her precise and thorough copy editing and for offering many crucial suggestions that have improved the manuscript. Thank you, Jennie, for your care with the stories, and for your literary prowess.

∽

I was raised in the warm bath of myths, rituals, symbols, and art. From my earliest memories I breathed in the fragrance of incense, and practiced on my tongue, the old grandmother of the romance languages—Latin. I was raised in the embrace of the Madonna. I was raised in the Roman Catholic Church.

Though I lived in profound dread that I might perish forever, yes forever, in hell—we were warned that by the *age of reason* (seven years of age) we were mature enough to commit a sin that could damn us for eternity—I nevertheless, loved the music, the candles, the statuary, the smell of the candle wax and, of course, the roar of the crowd—I was a performance level altar boy!

Catholicism, with its deep roots in the pantheistic beliefs of its early converts, has informed my storytelling. This old religion has been a kind of wrinkled and tattered map in the backpack of my soul that has predisposed me to love old stories, and sacred ritual—storytelling festivals, and wherever two are gathered together to listen and to tell.

∽

And, finally, thanks to Miles Davis for his "Blue in Green" melody that has kept me company for scores of lonely writing hours.

Appendix

Why Stories and Storytelling?

The roots of stories and storytelling are ancient—before humans learned to write, stories reminded them how to treat one another so that the tribe, and ultimately, the human race, could survive and flourish.

Plato's students in his *Republic* begin with the study of Myth.

Spiritual and religious traditions are transmitted through parables and narrative teachings.

"There have been great societies that have not used the wheel. There have been no societies that do not tell stories."—Ursula LeGuin

"The Old stories kept us from eating our grandchildren."—Emil Wolfgramm. Tongan Folklorist (at the NSN Pacific Region Storytelling Conference, Honolulu, Hawai'i. July 16-20, 2009, Waikiki)

We think in narrative: in images and sequential events, with our thought and memory laced with emotion. Stories and storytelling put these thoughts in cognitive and emotional context.

"The queen died, and then the king died. (facts) The queen died and the king died of a broken heart. (story)"—E. M. Forester

Virtually every life-long, intimate relationship is deepened and strengthened if we tell our loved one some or all of our life story.

Storytelling brings solace and joy to the soul, and health to the body. According to a controlled study by St. Olaf University, published in the Chicago Tribune (Spring, 2000), elders who told their life stories lowered their blood pressure.

Our culture still reveres this ancient tradition. When literary or cinema critics run out of superlatives they call a writer, film director, or playwright, a storyteller.

Storytelling is an effective persuasion skill and persuasion—advertising, counseling, consulting, and so on, is estimated to make up some 25% of GNP, which puts story and storytelling's worth at about $1 trillion a year to the US economy—*American Economic Review 85, 191-195 (1995).*

Earth Tales Recognized by a Restoration Ecologist

Ed Collins, Head of Restoration Ecology, McHenry County Conservations District, McHenry County, Illinois tells why storytelling matters:

Twenty-five years ago you came to Pleasant Valley and told stories one evening for a program I chaired. I had never met you nor did I know anything about "storytelling." Up to that point in my life, I had listened to older people tell stories in my family, not realizing that the stories were anything special to me—more like something old people did that—to be polite—the young had to sit through. The concept that a story had a life and possessed layers of meaning had never occurred to me. The story you told that night had an innate power to transform one's ideas—a power that I had never before witnessed. I watched your narrative steer the thinking of people in the audience and thought that a group or a whole culture could be influenced by a well-crafted story. It had never entered my mind.

All that changed during that evening.

While I have become an admirer of many of your stories, it was not the content so much as the profound epiphany that occurred in me that night as a result of listening that affected me. I was a very new naturalist then, focusing on the facts and data of ecology: names and uses of plants, ecological processes, niches, and other details were all-consuming to me. Listening to your stories that night opened a new path to me. I began to use your storytelling model as the way I informed people about the natural world, their place in it, and how they connect to one another and the stream of life we call nature. I have been on that path ever since. I guess you turned me into an ecological storyteller, and I can trace that change, that direction, precisely to that night.

Eulogy for Duncan Williamson

I'm honoured and grateful to have been asked by Linda to say a few words about my dear friend Duncan on behalf of the storytelling community, who so loved him and were so inspired by him.

It's very difficult in a few words to give a sense of the depth and breadth of Duncan's gift to the storytelling world.

First of all there's the inexhaustible repertoire, the three thousand or so stories, the ballads, the poems, the jokes, the riddles, the anecdotes ... absorbed and remembered from a lifetime of encounters.

From earliest childhood he was soaking up stories and songs like bread dipped into gravy. It was his father, his uncles and most of all his two grannies Wee Belle the storyteller and big Bet McColl the ballad singer who inspired him to remember everything he heard. When he left home at fourteen his ear was tuned to the repertoires of fishermen, dry-stone wallers, farm hands, travellers ... he told, sang and listened at ceilidhs and camp-fires the length and breadth of Scotland (and later the world) learning from everyone he met ... and giving as good as he got. It was a repertoire that was still being added to up to the last months of his life.

This phenomenal body of remembered tradition would be remarkable in itself ... but to it must be added Duncan's artistry.

Everything he heard, saw, touched, smelt, tasted and felt added flavour to the bubbling stew of stories he kept in his memory. He'd lived an extraordinary life to the full. He'd known how it was to be starving hungry, to be kept awake all night by seals with tooth-ache, to fit a cast-off horse-shoe, to guddle for trout. He'd experienced loss and love and the pleasures of good company, he'd trodden the roads of Scotland over and over... all this fed into his stories, giving them substance, sympathy, humour, a grounding in real places and all the insights that come from a life of hard graft and sharp, humane observation. He might be telling a Jack tale, a Silkie story, a Joke ... but in his imagination it always rested on a solid core of real lived experience that made the story true.

Also, through his vast inner store of ballads and poems, through his knowledge of Gaelic and Cant, he had a rich and rare vocabulary and a deep feel for the music of language.

He was, quite simply, the greatest bearer of stories and songs in the Scots and English language.

But there's something more, all this meant nothing to Duncan unless it was given away. With stories and songs (as with everything else) he gave freely, insisting that once you'd heard it, it was yours to tell again.

With the sequence of wonderful books he wrote with Linda, and with the recordings that have been made of him, his unique voice has reached the four corners of the world ... and will continue to do so. Countless people, people he never met, are telling his stories.

Nothing could have pleased him more.

But it was in his delightful, mischievous, welcoming, heartfelt company that they had their richest life—and that, we've lost forever.

Nobody can be feeling that more strongly than Duncan's family, to whom we extend our deepest sympathy and love.

And as we sit here we might catch a glimpse, out of the corners of our eyes, of a host of luminous presences ... among whom there are Silkies, Old Father Time, Donald Archie Dougal, Douglas MacLean, A Hunchback and a Swan, a White Snake, the Flying Horse of Earthdom, a battery of Hen-Wives, Thomas the Rhymer, Captain Wedderburn, assorted Factors, Posties, Farmers and Fishermen, an Oyster Girl, the Devil and his Grandmother, a Lighthouse Keeper, many Marys, Hedgehurst, the Laird o' Drum, several castles full of kings (one with a thorn in his foot), the Broonie, many Tramps and a Taxman or two—all of whom have doffed their caps and are kneeling in great silence ... and the chief mourner is Jack.

> —Thanks to authors Hugh Lupton and Ben Haggarty for their permission to reprint Duncan Williamson's eulogy.

Notes

1. Auden, W. H. *As I Walked out One Evening* (poem)

2. Merton, Thomas (1915-1968). Victor A. Kramer is the founding editor of *The Merton Annual* and a coeditor of *The Complete Journal of Thomas Merton, Volume Four*. He has been engaged in Merton-related studies for 30 years. Kramer has cited three books in particular that demonstrate "the significant changes in awareness" in Merton's writing. The first of these books, 1949's *Seeds of Contemplation*, is entirely spiritual in focus. *New Seeds of Contemplation*, published in 1961 as a revised version of the same book, reflects what Kramer called Merton's "greater concern for the problems of living in the world." The third book, 1964's *Seeds of Destruction*, is a collection of essays on world problems, including racism. According to Kramer, the changing themes illustrated in these three books reflect Merton's movement from solitary monk in a monastery cell to social activist. See also *Passion for Peace: The Social Essays*, edited by William Henry Shannon, Crossroad Publishing (New York, NY), 1995.

3. Williamson, Duncan, see *The Thorn In The King's Foot*; see also Williamson, Duncan, 1994 *The Horsieman, Memories Of A Traveller 1928-1958*, also his obituary in the Guardian: http://www.theguardian.com/news/2007/nov/22/guardianobituaries.obituaries1

4. The late Ray Hicks is considered the patriarch of Appalachian Storytelling. See his long time friend and colleague, Connie Regan Blake's website, http://www.storywindow.com/tribute.htm for a tribute to Ray Hicks. Also citations on Appalachian storytelling tradition of Beech Mountain, North Carolina.

5. Laura Simms, one of the founders of the American storytelling revival. Storyteller, writer, educator, peace and justice advocate, she has been a Senior Research Fellow for the International Peace Institute at Rutgers University-Newark under the auspices of UNESCO. See more at: http://www.laurasimms.com/short-bio/#sthash.3CfaGvCm.dpuf

6. http://www.gioiatimpanelli.com/; "No one in the world, yes the world, can tell a story like Joia Timpanelli."—Frank McCourt.

7. Robert Bly, groundbreaking poet, editor, translator, storyteller, and father

of what he has called "the expressive men's movement,"
http://robertbly.com/

Chapter 1

1. Be not afraid (story) ... I am not sure where I first heard this story, but I'm sure it is traditional. I had forgotten that I had told it until I recently heard storyteller, Bill Harley, mention it in a keynote he was giving at the National Storytelling Network Conference in San Antonio, 2012. He recounted that he had heard it from me. After some 30 yrs of seeking out, hearing, and telling thousands of stories, the origins sometimes blur. But there is a kind of critical intuition that tries to judge authenticity—is there a truth in the story that would have been worth preserving over the millennia? I think this simple story of courage and recognition of the importance of naming our demons meets that test.

2. A story from the Hassidic tradition that I learned from the telling of Corrine Stavish. http://jf.md/witnessvideo; See her book, *Seeds from Our Past: Planting for the Future: Jewish Stories and Folktales* Paperback. Oct 1997. Ed, Corinne Stavish.

3. An initiation is some event that takes us deeper into life than we would normally go. It may be a hardship (death of a loved one) or a joyous occasion (birth of a baby). But it always dictates a new direction in life, and new territory to be traveled, demons to be tamed, and mentors to seek out. See Meade, Michael; *Men And The Water Of Life.*

Chapter 2

1. Greater Prairie Chicken: see this beautiful and endangered species "performing" its mating display at
https://www.youtube.com/watch?v=vOuVAfyk4o8

2. The Métis: Canada: http://www.thecanadianencyclopedia.ca/en/article/metis/ Métis are people of mixed European and Indigenous ancestry, and one of the three recognized Aboriginal peoples in Canada. They originated largely in Western Canada and emerged as a political force in the 19th century, radiating outwards from the Red River Settlement.

3. See: "Kathryn T. Windham, a Storyteller of the South, Dies at 93". http://www.nytimes.com/2011/06/16/books/kathryn-tucker-windham-southern-storyteller-dies-at-93.html?_r=0

4. Appalachian Storytellers. See notes on Jack Tellers of Beech Mountain, NC.

5. The McGuffey Readers, http://mcguffeyreaders.com/history.htm
   Two of the best-known school books in the history of American education were the 18th century New England Primer and the 19th century McGuffey Readers. Of the two, McGuffey's was the most popular and widely used. It is estimated that at least 120 million copies of McGuffey's Readers were sold between 1836 and 1960, placing its sales in a category with the Bible and Webster's Dictionary.

6. "Soldier Jack" is the last story in *Jack Tales*, a collection of 18 stories collected by Richard Chase during the Great Depression-era Federal Writers' Project. Chase collected most of the stories from the Hicks, Harmon, and Ward families.

Chapter 3

1 Johnny Moses is a master storyteller, traditional healer, and respected spiritual leader who carries the medicine teachings of his Northwest Coast ancestors. Born at Ohiat, a remote Nuu-chah-nulth (Nootka) village on the west coast of Vancouver Island, British Columbia, Moses has a multi-tribal ancestry, which includes the Nuu-chah-nulth, Saanich, Snohomish, Duwamish, and Chehamus peoples (Originally printed in *Shaman's Drum* magazine, Spring 1991.) Re-printed by permission. *Shaman's Drum* is the world's leading magazine dealing with experiential shamanism and transformative spirituality. Write Shaman's Drum, P.O. Box 270, Williams, Oregon 97544, USA; or, call (541) 846-1313

2. See Eleanor Roosevelt: http://theboldlife.com/2014/04/27-courageous-quotes-from-eleanor-roosevelt-to-inspire-you-2-specials/

3. "The Story of the Cracked Pot," http://www.sacinandanaswami.com/en/s1a38/wisdom-stories/the-cracked-water-pot.html

4. For the history of the Illinois Holocaust Museum and Education Center see: http://www.ilholocaustmuseum.org/
   Lisa Derman, Holocaust survivor and past president of the Illinois Holocaust Memorial and Education Center died of a heart attack while telling her story at the Illinois Storytelling Festival (2002). See documentary filmed that day: http://www.springrovevillage.com/parks-recreation-and-sports/lisa-derman-memorial-at-spring-grove-park

5. For John Lennon quote see http://www.quotationspage.com /quote/571.html

6. I learned this story from Laura Simms; also see *Buber, Martin: Tales of the Hasidim: The Early Masters*. New York, Schocken Books, 1947, also *The Story of The Baal Shem: Life, Love And Teachings Of The Founder Of The Chassidim And Jewish Mysticism* by Dr. J. L. Snitzer. Translated by Dr. Samuel Rosenblatt New York, Pardes Publishing House, 1947.

7. "The Man Who's Horse Ran Off," see *Wisdom Tales*, Heather Forest, (August House, 2005).

Chapter 4

1. Third eye: speculative invisible eye which provides perception beyond ordinary ... see "What is the Third Eye?": http://personaltao.com /teachings/shamanic/about-visions/what-is-the-third-eye/

2. "The Peddler of Swaffham." I first heard Jay O'Callahan tell this story on his powerful Master Class DVD available on www.ocallahan .com. I then heard Elizabeth Ellis tell the same story and was struck by the love that the peddler had for children in her version. See *English Fairy and Other Folk Tales*; p.76-77; by Hartland, Edwin Sidney.

3. The English Blackbird is a thrush and a beautiful singer. See and hear one at: https://www.youtube.com/watch?v=997RTKzc39c

4. Kristin Olson-Huddle is a storyteller and author and has generously granted permission to reprint her powerful and tender story.

5. See *Is God the Only Reality? Science Points to a Deeper Meaning of the Universe*, Templeton and Herrmann (1994).

Chapter 5

1. Signal Trees: Native Americans bent small saplings to mark trails. Trees grew and became landmark trail guides. http://www. oldeforester.com/Sigtree.html. Trail signal trees are extremely important historically. Native Americans made them by bending a sapling and holding it by some means until the first curve was fixed by growth.

2. Jack Tale Tellers of Beech Mountain, see: Carden, Kara. "Hicks, Ray (1922-2003) Storyteller." *Encyclopedia of Appalachia*. Knoxville: The University of Tennessee Press, 2006. pps.1249-1250.

Leonard, Robert H. "Performing Arts." *Encyclopedia of Appalachia.* Knoxville: The University of Tennessee Press, 2006. pp. 1225-1228.

Lightfoot, William. "Hicks-Harmon Families." *Folklore: An Encyclopedia.* New York and London: Garland Publishing, Inc., 1996. pp. 367-369.

Brunvand, Jan Harold, ed. "Ward, Marshall (1906-1981)." *American Folklore: An Encyclopedia.* New York and London: Garland Publishing, Inc., 1996. pp. 739-740.

Perdue, Charles L., Jr. "Chase, Richard (1904-1988)." *American Folklore: An Encyclopedia.* New York and London: Garland Publishing, Inc., 1996.

3. See Folk Legacy Records, Ray Hicks Album: http://www.folk-legacy .com/store/Scripts/prodView.asp?idproduct=38

4. Jackie Torrence, a pioneer in the American revival of storytelling. One of the first to travel widely and appear on Television (*NBC Late Night With David Letterman*), see obituary in the *Los Angeles Times* http://articles.latimes.com/2004/dec/12/local/me-torrence12

5. See: Studs Terkel's books, *Working, and Division Street: America* (Racism in Chicago), also radio archives: http://studsterkel.org/:

6. Inez Ashdown, historian of Maui County, see: http://apps.ksbe.edu /kaiwakiloumoku/ola-na-iwi/inez_ashdown. I met with Inez on several storytelling trips to Hawai'i. She was an example of the many who came to the islands from all over the globe and fell completely in love with Hawai'i's history and culture.

Chapter 6

1. Buber, Martin, *Tales of the Hasidim: The Early Masters* (New York, Schocken Books, 1947) and *The Story of The Baal Shem: Life, Love And Teachings Of The Founder Of The Chassidim And Jewish Mysticism* by Dr. J. L. Snitzer.

2. Wolpert, Stanley. *Gandhi's Passion: The Life and Legacy of Mahatma Gandhi*, (Oxford University Press, 2002) pg. 197 .

3. Hart, B. H. Liddell, *The Rommel Papers* (1953); Horne, Alistair, *To Lose a Battle, France: 1940* (1969), see also: http://www.eyewitnesstohistory.com/blitzkrieg.htm

4. Geronimo—see Debo, Angie, *Geronimo: The Man, His Time, His Place* (1976)

5. See image "Three dead Americans lie on the beach at Buna" at https://iconicphotos.wordpress.com/2009/07/24/three-dead-americans-lie-on-the-beach-at-buna/

6. "The War Photo No One Would Publish". When Kenneth Jarecke photographed an Iraqi man burned alive, he thought it would change the way Americans saw the Gulf War. But the media wouldn't run the picture. From http://www.theatlantic.com/features/archive/2014/08/the-war-photo-no-one-would-publish/375762/?google_editors_picks=true

7. Excerpt from "The Question," by Rumi, see *The Essential Rumi*, Translations by Coleman Barks with John Moyne (1995) for the complete work.

8. The term "Soldier's Heart" was first coined in the post-Civil War era when people were looking at these ... veterans returning from Civil War combat and trying to understand why they had been changed. There was general recognition that they had been changed, and that many of those changes were not for the good. See http://www.pbs.org/wgbh/pages/frontline/shows/heart/themes/shellshock.html

9. *War and the Soul: Healing Our Nation's Veterans from Post-Traumatic Stress Disorder* by Edward Tick PhD Tick's methods draw on compelling case studies and ancient warrior traditions worldwide to restore the soul so that the veteran can truly come home to community, family, and self.

10. *Continuities in Cultural Evolution*, Margaret Mead, first published in 1964.

Chapter 7

1. For information regarding the pagan celebration of Samhain see: http://paganwiccan.about.com/od/samhainoctober31/p/Samhain_History.htm

2. In Mexican folk tradition, the female personification of death.

Chapter 8

1. Troyes, Chretin. 1999 (paperback). *The Story Of The Grail* (Chretien de Troyes Romances S) This was my most important source for the Percival story in this text.

Bibliography

Campbell, Joseph. *The Hero With A Thousand Faces*. New York: Pantheon
   Books, 1948.
   Campbell's magnum opus in which he documents the heroic
   story that appears in virtually all world mythology. George Lucas
   founded the Joseph Campbell Society in honor of the man whose
   work inspired Lucas' fantasy franchise: STAR WARS.

Chase, Richard. *Jack Tales*. New York: Houghton Mifflin, 1943.
   Collected in the Southern Appalachian Mountains during the
   Federal Writers' Project—a folk and cultural treasure. The Hicks
   family is mentioned in the introduction.

Chase, Richard. *Grandfather Tales*, Boston: Houghton Mifflin, 1948.
   This is a must read. More Appalachian folk tales collected from
   living tradition bearers.

Estés, Clarissa Pinkola. *Women Who Run With The Wolves*. New York:
   Ballantine Books, 1992.
   Another classic. Estés explores the feminine and masculine in
   mythology with breathtaking depth and skill. Like Campbell's
   work, it digests better in small bites. I have found this collection to
   be rich in stories and commentary. A must read.

Jung, Carl. *Memories, Dreams, and Reflections*. New York: Pantheon
   Books, 1963.
   Jung has long been considered the storyteller's psychologist. His
   work has been groundbreaking in the area of myth, archetype,
   dreams and symbolism.

Hillman, James. *The Force of Character and the Lasting Life*. New York:
   Random House, 1999.
   Anyone working with elders or hoping to understand the aging
   process for themselves must read this book. It will raise your spirit,
   ground you at your time of life and help you to look outward to
   make your mark on the world as a wise elder/wisdom keeper.

Lane, Belden. *The Solace Of Fierce Landscapes*. New York: Oxford
   University Press, 1998.

Dr. Lane is a theologian as well as a storyteller. He examines the roots of story and storytelling in the Judeo-Christian tradition. In this volume his "fierce landscapes" range from his vigil beside his mother's death bed to the rigors of the desert fathers and mothers in the Sinai.

May, Rollo. *The Cry For Myth*. New York: W. W. Norton & Company Inc., 1991.
May looks at the psychological aspects of myth, both for individuals and societies. He sees myth as more necessary than ever as traditional institutions and mores break down.

McCarthy, Bernard. *Jack In Two Worlds*. Chapel Hill: University of North Carolina Press, 1994.
This is a carefully researched tome on the traditional tellers of Jack Tales with the tales themselves transcribed word for word. Very complete bibliography for further reading.

Meade, Michael. *Men and The Water of Life*. New York: Harper Collins, 1993.
Storyteller, poet, mythologist Michael Meade is a must-read for every man, as well as for every woman who wants to understand men. If we men were as introspective as women, this book would have been a best-seller like *Women Who Run With The Wolves*. It is a particularly strong look at young men who have been left behind and not mentored by older, mature men. Meade argues that young men need to be initiated into a deeper understanding of their role in our culture and in their own manhood.

Pink, Daniel. *A Whole New Mind: Why Right-Brainers Will Rule The Future*. New York: Riverhead Books, 2005.
Pink lists several skills that will be needed to prosper in the twenty-first century. Storytelling is one of the skills that he says will "... rule the next century." Great applications for corporate cultures and anyone interested in how stories are used in persuasion.

Rinpoche, Sogyal. *The Tibetan Book Of Living And Dying*. San Francisco: Harper San Francisco, 1994.
A deeply spiritual book that is an exposition of the Buddhist view of death as well as a guide for anyone who is dying or supporting a dying person. Beautifully written, comforting, and filled with practical and compassionate advice. I found it a God-send when I was a caretaker for my sister in hospice.

Shenk, Joshua Wolf. *Lincoln's Melancholy*. New York: Houghton Mifflin, 2005.
Shenk documents Lincoln's depression and proposes that it was his familiarity with his own pain and darkness that made him such a brilliant, compassionate leader, and an abolitionist.

Sawyer, Ruth. *The Way Of The Storyteller*. New York: Viking Press, 1942.
The first book that I ever read about Storytelling. Ruth Sawyer was one of the first in modern times to travel the world telling and collecting stories. Her plea to maintain storytelling as a folk art is critical to a thorough understanding of the craft and pitfalls of performance.

Sher, Gail. *One Continuous Mistake: Four Noble Truths For Writers*. New York: Penguin Books, 1999.
The most important and helpful book on writing that I have found. An inspiring book for any writer, with exercises as well as new perspectives on being a writer. The four noble truths: (1) Writers write, (2) Writing is a practice, (3) you don't know what your writing until you are done, (4) If writing is a practice, the only way to fail is not to write.

Sobol, Joseph. *The Storytellers Journey*. Urbana: University of Illinois Press, 1999.
Dr. Joseph Sobol, PhD, takes the reader through the birth, growth, and transformation of the storytelling community over a 25 year period (1974-1999). Historically, storytellers played an important role in many cultures, as those who kept the traditions, customs, myths and legends of the group alive through oral tradition. This is the best account of the history of America's storytelling revival. A tour de force.

Troyes, Chretien. *The Story Of The Grail* (Chretien de Troyes Romances S). New Haven: Yale University Press, 1999.
This was my most important source for the Percival story in this text.

Williamson, Duncan. *The Horsieman: Memories of a Traveller 1928-58*. Edinburgh: Birlinn Limited, 1994
Duncan Williamson was both one of the last and best known of Scotland's Traveller storytellers. This autobiography tells for the first time, his own story of his life as a Traveller, hawking his wares, collecting stories, and travelling through Scotland.

If you have enjoyed Jim May's stories,
please take some time to visit:

www.jimmaystoryteller.com
www.parkhurstbrothers.com
www.storynet.org